The Seattle
Book of Dates

ttle

Book of Dates

Adventures, Escapes, and Secret Spots

EDEN DAWN
ASHOD SIMONIAN

SASQUATCH BOOKS
SEATTLE

Copyright © 2023 by Eden Dawn and Ashod Simonian

Printed in China

SASQUATCH BOOKS with colophon is a registered trademark of Penguin Random House LLC

27 26 25 24 23   9 8 7 6 5 4 3 2 1

Editor: Jen Worick
Production editor: Isabella Hardie
Production designer: Tony Ong
Illustrations: Ashod Simonian

Library of Congress Cataloging-in-Publication Data

Names: Dawn, Eden, author. | Simonian, Ashod, author.
Title: The Seattle book of dates : adventures, escapes, and secret spots /
Eden Dawn and Ashod Simonian ; illustrations: Ashod Simonian.
Description: Seattle : Sasquatch Books, [2023] | Includes index. | Summary:
"A stylish, design-y, cheeky, curated guidebook of cool places for
Seattleites to go on dates/outings/field trips/adventures. These range
from 1-hour coffee and ice cream dates to multi-day expeditions around
Washington state (and Vancouver)" -- Provided by publisher.
Identifiers: LCCN 2023001262 | ISBN 9781632174314 (paperback) | ISBN
9781632174321 (ebook)
Subjects: LCSH: Seattle (Wash.)--Guidebooks. | Seattle Region
(Wash.)--Guidebooks. | Dating (Social customs)--Washington
(State)--Seattle. | Dating (Social customs)--Washington (State)--Seattle
Region.
Classification: LCC F899.S43 D37 2023 | DDC
979.7/77204934--dc23/eng/20230120
LC record available at https://lccn.loc.gov/2023001262

ISBN: 978-1-63217-431-4

Sasquatch Books
1325 Fourth Avenue, Suite 1025
Seattle, WA 98101

SasquatchBooks.com

MIX
Paper | Supporting
responsible forestry
FSC® C008047
FSC
www.fsc.org

To my current husband,
Ashod, and to my future
husband, Eddie Vedder.

To my current wife, Eden,
and to all my future cats.

ZONE 1

DOWNTOWN,
SOUTH LAKE UNION,
MAGNOLIA, QUEEN ANNE
2

PIONEER SQUARE,
INTERNATIONAL DISTRICT
8

CAPITOL HILL, PIKE, PINE,
MADISON, MADRONA
13

U-DISTRICT
18

FREMONT, WALLINGFORD,
NORTH LAKE
23

BALLARD
30

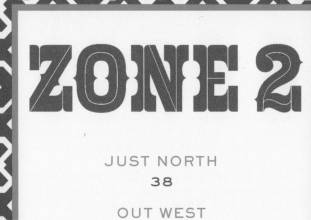

ZONE 2

JUST NORTH
38

OUT WEST
42

EAST SIDE
45

DOWN SOUTH
50

ZONE 3

TAC-TOWN
58

SOUTH OF THE BORDER
66

ISLANDS OF THE NORTH
72

ISLANDS OF THE SOUTH
83

ZONE 4

VANCOUVER
90

NORTH CASCADES
96

TOUR DE FORESTS
100

MOUNT RAINIER
106

OLYMPIA
110

ZONE 5

SEA TO SKY
116

EASTERN WASHINGTON
121

PORTLAND
125

OLYMPIC LOOP
130

ROYAL ISLE
136

ACKNOWLEDGMENTS
145

CHEAT SHEET
147

INDEX
153

An imperfect but, hopefully, helpful map

• WHISTLER

• VANCOUVER

• BELLINGHAM
• ORCAS

VICTORIA •

FORKS •

SEATTLE

• TACOMA

• OLYMPIA

MT. RAINIER •

• PORTLAND

ZONE 1

DOWNTOWN/SOUTH LAKE UNION
MAGNOLIA/QUEEN ANNE, PIONEER SQUARE/
INTERNATIONAL DISTRICT, CAPITOL HILL/
PIKE/PINE/MADISON/MADRONA,
U-DISTRICT, FREMONT/WALLINGFORD
NORTH LAKE, BALLARD

ZONE 2

JUST NORTH, OUT WEST,
EAST SIDE, DOWN SOUTH

WINTHROP

ZONE 3

TAC-TOWN,
SOUTH OF THE BORDER,
ISLANDS OF THE NORTH,
ISLANDS OF THE SOUTH

LEAVENWORTH

YAKIMA

ZONE 4

VANCOUVER, NORTH CASCADES,
TOUR DE FORESTS, MT. RAINIER, OLYMPIA

WALLA WALLA •

ZONE 5

SEA TO SKY, EASTERN WASHINGTON,
PORTLAND, OLYMPIC LOOP, ROYAL ISLE

Introduction

Way back in the pre-pandemic glow of 2018, while out on one of our fun weekend adventures we hatched the idea for *The Portland Book of Dates*. Eden has lived in Oregon her whole life and spent her career as a journalist writing about the city, while Ashod moved to Portland in 2006 after passing through on countless tours with one of his many bands. The ensuing two years were a flurry of adventures under the guise of "research." Then, just as we were sending the final files off to the printer, Covid changed everything.

We sat at home, riddled with anxiety for the world, for the people and places we loved, and wondered if all our hard work had gone to waste. The book came out early in 2021, along with the glimmer of hope that the lives we all remembered would return. We had a virtual book launch party with three hundred viewers, discovering that people were eager to head back out into the city, and our little baby book started flying off the shelves. We were reminded that the world is always changing, favorite haunts coming and going all the time, and to support and celebrate the places you love while you can.

When our dear friends at Sasquatch approached us a few months later with the idea of doing *The Seattle Book of Dates*, we were maybe a little naive about the pandemic being over (and, as two extroverted Leos, also starved for attention). Ashod knew the city well from spending a bunch of time here in his Seattle-based band Preston School of Industry, and Eden has spent years sleeping on the floors of seemingly every dorm at UW, at couches across Capitol Hill, and later in nice guest rooms as her childhood bestie moved here right after high school. Together, we tapped our years of time spent here and our bevy of Washingtonian friends who let us mine them for details during research trips.

We immediately booked a small cabin on the Hood Canal for the first of what would be many excursions around the state. We spent birthdays at Lake Crescent, sipping martinis in Adirondacks on the lodge's porch, and in Leavenworth, floating through that fairy-tale town on inner tubes. Eden had her first ever public nap in a hammock at Scandinave Spa in Whistler, and Ashod took a walk down memory lane in Olympic National Park, where his uncle was a ranger in the 1980s. There are too many missed ferries and sunsets over the Sound to count. We won't miss the hours on I-5, but it is strangely emotional to see this chapter coming to a close.

In May of 2016, Ashod took a knee next to a fluorescent waterfall deep in the recesses of the mine in the Seven Dwarfs' House at Oregon's most off-the-wall amusement park, Enchanted Forest, and we've just celebrated ten years since first laying eyes on each other. Our love has always been infused with an appreciation for all things kitsch, and the dates in this book are no exception. From tropical speakeasies to mossy hobbit houses, we left no stone unturned in our mission to find the most fun and unexpected ways to spend time together.

The Pacific Northwest is wild, stunning, and strange, and every day we feel fortunate to not only call this place home but to have found each other within it. We wish nothing but magic to you and yours as you continue to explore every nook and cranny this great region has to offer.

WITH LOVE & FOR LOVE,

Eden & Ashod

ZONE 1
In the City

TO EVERETT

TO KENMORE

Ballard

Fremont,
Wallingford,
North Lake

U-District

TO BELLEVUE →

Downtown,
South Lake Union,
Magnolia,
Queen Anne

Capitol Hill,
Pike/Pine,
Madison,
Madrona

TO TACOMA

TO ISSAQUAH →

Pioneer Square,
International District

Downtown • South Lake Union • Magnolia • Queen Anne

Ah, downtown. The heart of the city! The height of the city! There are the things you know, like the famous Pike Place Market, the sky-high office buildings, and the eagle-eyed parking meter patrol. But it is also a place to eat romantic meals and take in shows. A place to sweat out your stresses, hop on the water, and stroll with treats in hand.

LET'S FRENCH

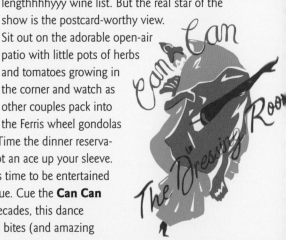

At some point, all cozy couples hit a pivotal milestone: the day they first French. We are, of course, talking about dining and entertainment from the country so known for romance, they named intertwining tongues after it. *Allons-y!* Begin the evening by following the glowing red neon lights in Pike Place toward **Maximilien restaurant.**

   Owner operated since 1997, this little bistro oozes with classic date magic from the white linen tablecloths and flowers on the table to the lengthhhhyyy wine list. But the real star of the show is the postcard-worthy view. Sit out on the adorable open-air patio with little pots of herbs and tomatoes growing in the corner and watch as other couples pack into the Ferris wheel gondolas below or barges steam on by. Time the dinner reservation with sunset and you've got an ace up your sleeve.

   Post frites and Niçoise, it's time to be entertained by the venerable art of burlesque. Cue the **Can Can Culinary Cabaret!** For two decades, this dance theater has served up delicious bites (and amazing beignets if you're in the mood) inside their plush red velvet den. Once nestled into your seat, the show begins with dancers strutting the stage, demonstrating fantastic choreographed routines and feats of flexibility—all while wearing little more than rhinestones and ruffles. It's sexy and sassy, while also feeling sweet and fun. Four words to sum up a *rendez-vous romantique*.

THE BIG O

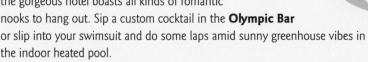

We are big fans of the staycation. The fun of vacation—hotel romps, coffee in bed, and nary a dirty dish to clean—all without the lengthy travel time. For a classy-ass time, check into the historic **Fairmont Olympic Hotel**. Opened since 1924, and on the former site of U-Dub's first campus, the gorgeous hotel boasts all kinds of romantic nooks to hang out. Sip a custom cocktail in the **Olympic Bar** or slip into your swimsuit and do some laps amid sunny greenhouse vibes in the indoor heated pool.

Venture out of your bathrobes for some culture at a tried-and-true stalwart we can easily take for granted. Spend some time at the famed floating glass platform architectural wonder of the **Central Library**, home to 1.5 million books you can comb through together (pop into the visually stunning **Red Hall** on the fourth floor if you're able). Each of you should reveal your all-time favorite page-turner to the other and then carry your conversation over to the **Bathtub Gin & Co**. The doorway to the speakeasy is in a back alleyway that leads down into a cozy little den, the perfect spot to share your deepest thoughts on *Howl's Moving Castle* or *A Wrinkle in Time*.

HOT TIP: When winter SAD hits hard and you need some light, play one of the library's many stockpiled games under a skylight for some free vitamin D.

WILL YOU BE MY SWEATHEART?

We all know the way to cope with PNW winters: find a way to warm them bones up. Enter **Banya 5**. At this all-gender Russian bathhouse, melt off winter inside the 220-degree brick sauna. Semi-bake the bod until you're a sweaty mess and then hop into the 55-degree cold plunge for the freezing thrill of a lifetime, followed by a soak in the lukewarm salt pool. Rinse and repeat. Truly go for it with the **Venik Night**, where you batter your body with soaked oak leaves as part of the fun!

Post plunge, you'll be famished, which means the time has come to visit **Skalka** for khachapuri, aka bread boats! Don't let the simple eastern European menu fool you. Choosing between the smattering of hand-stretched baked-to-order lovelies overflowing with eggs, cheese, and oh so much more will be exceedingly difficult. Load those bellies up and snuggle on the couch together for the nap of your lives.

MOONRISE KINGDOM

Here's a sweet one (literally) that's as cheap as can be. Skip into the Queen Anne **Molly Moon** with childlike glee and get a cone of Yeti ice cream. FYI: The single scoop is baseball sized, but you can also get the golf-ball-size kids' scoop. Then walk the three blocks down to **Kerry Park** for the perfect view of the city as the sun starts to set and the moon comes up. You can ogle the ferries coming in, the Space Needle from a new angle, the beauty of Alki—all while someone randomly does capoeira in the park besides you while you slurp.

Before you leave, take a short walk down Highland Drive to **Parsons Garden**, which was originally the family garden of fancy man Reginald H. Parsons. In 1956, the clan gave up their expansive front yard to the city for a public park. Open every day during daylight hours, the pocket park features rickety benches to rest and lick any remnants of your cone, tucked away amid beautiful crooked trees. It's also a particularly lovely place for wedding ceremonies if that sort of information is useful to you and your sweetheart.

OLD-FASHIONED FUN

How to tackle the age-old dilemma: Consume carbs or take to the water? The only solution is, of course, to do both. First, grab another couple or two, as this is best done in a group, then pay a visit to an old fave: the flagship location of **Top Pot**. Since 2002, this hometown doughnut chain has been keeping us sugar hyped with their cult-favorite Feather Boa (fancy coconut shavings act as "feathers"), but we implore you to give the classic glazed Old Fashioned and a cup of coffee combo a go.

Once you're properly buzzing on sugar and caffeine, work out those twitchy muscles by hopping on a stand-up paddleboard rental from **Moss Bay**. For an affordable hourly rate, you and your crew can use the ol' biceps and core to work your way through sheltered (i.e., chill) waterways to ogle houseboats and enjoy the sunshine.

But what if it isn't SUP weather? No worries, this is a two-sided coin of a date. Still get your Top Pot fix (this time hit the Queen Anne location) and enjoy a scenic soak in a **Hot Tub Boat**. The stellar notion of hot-tub-meets-boat came to be in 2011, and now the local biz has a small fleet available to rent. No fancy training is needed for this slow-boating beauty (which tops out at five miles per hour) operated by joystick—just the desire to soak, sightsee, and slay the gray.

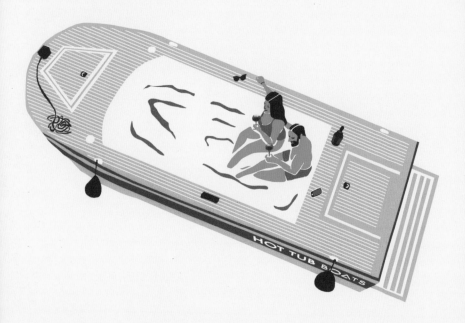

More Fun

THE ART OF MAKING OUT—Everyone knows museums are a great spot for dates, especially on a rainy day, but **Seattle Art Museum** deserves a special mention for its forward-thinking programming and emphasis on culturally relevant but oft-overlooked music, fashion, and outsider art exhibits.

GREASE THE WHEELS—If you're looking to send a message to your date that you are unpretentious but still have a taste for the most pristine ingredients, ask them to meet you at **Jack's Fish Spot and Crab Pot** in Pike Place Market. Nothing screams easygoing like the willingness to be a tourist in your own city. Squeeze onto stools at the tiny metal bar and take in the sensory overload of sights, sounds, smells, and—most importantly—tastes of this crowded yet somehow still hidden gem.

SIR MIX-A-LATTE—It's hard to believe **KEXP** has been serving the music lovers of this city for more than fifty years. In 2015, they moved to hip, modern digs on the edge of Seattle Center and added a public viewing space for live in-studio performances. Plan your date correctly and you can meet in the studio's airy gathering space for coffee at **Caffe Vita** before catching an intimate, one-of-a-kind show by one of your favorite artists.

BELLY LAUGHS—If you prefer your hummus with a little bit of jiggle, pull up a pouf Wednesday through Sunday at Belltown's **Marrakesh** for tableside rosewater handwashing, acrobatic tea pouring, and a feast fit for a sultan while chiffon and rhinestone-clad belly dancers shake it like a Polaroid picture.

Pioneer Square •
International District

Within Seattle's first neighborhood, settled in 1852, and the neighboring International District (ID), you'll find a lovely mix of old and new, familiar and first time. Indulge in centuries-old recipes while sipping on just-invented craft cocktails, or take in some sportsball with a banh mi in hand. Whatever you do, give yourselves some time to stray from the course because the nooks and crannies of this part of town are full of treasures waiting to be discovered.

GET HIGH ON HISTORY!

Got parents visiting? This is the kind of day dads dream of! Begin at **Klondike Gold Rush National Historic Park**. Don't let the fact that it's a national park fool you—this isn't a forest, but one of their four hundred "parks" that cover cultural and national heritage. In this case, heritage about getting that thar gold! There are gold bars, historic artifacts, and stories of famous Seattleites (Hello John W. Nordstrom and your stylish goods!). It's free and worth the pop in to lay the mental groundwork for how the city changed so quickly.

It also dovetails perfectly to your next stop, the **Smith Tower Observatory**, Seattle's original skyscraper and observation deck. Completed in 1914, the 484-foot pyramid-topped tower was instigated by fancy businessman Lyman Cornelius Smith when financial interest in Seattle was "so hot right now" because of the gold rush. Once the spiffy tower was built, it remained the tallest building on the West Coast for nearly fifty years until a certain other Seattle icon (cough cough Space Needle) needed the attention more.

Pay the fee to ride the century-plus Otis elevators up to the thirty-fifth-floor observation deck. Sip on a perfectly made old fashioned in the Prohibition-style speakeasy, **Smith Tower Observatory Bar**, where the bartender might tell you the tale about how back in the day there was a police lieutenant named Big Boy Roy (catchy!) in the building who ran a bootlegging operation out

of the tower during Prohibition and used a radio system to not get caught. Then take in the view—as stunning as they come—with your totally legal cocktail and be glad the days of Prohibition are behind us.

WOO YOUR DATE

The success of a good date can be summed up in one vital word: snacks. That might even be better when said snack is a fluffy, soft pastry that smells of hot butter and joy. Find that by popping into the unassuming storefront of **Cake House**, where the small, family-owned business has served up authentic Hong Kong–style pastries for the last thirty years. Bring cash to snap up the taro or red bean paste buns made from the softest brioche dough. Or maybe the coconut buns. Or maybe the glistening fruit tarts. Or maybe all of it.

Take your highly affordable haul up to the mini-Eden at the **Danny Woo Community Garden**. The special 1.5-acre garden is a growing space for more than seventy low-income, elder gardeners from the area (the average gardener's age is almost eighty years old!). Wander around the space and take in their combined decades of expertise, from the carefully pruned fruit trees to the specialty produce to the flock of chickens hanging out. In addition to being an important part of supporting the elder community, the lovely gardens also serve as an outdoor classroom for kids to encourage that #gardeninglife early. The garden also hosts multiple volunteer days throughout the year where they ask folks for help, a great (and fulfilling) date in itself.

LET'S HAVE A BALL

Ah, America's pastime. No, not that. We're talking about baseball! But the beauty of the game is that it requires little to no effort or knowledge to appreciate watching someone swagger up to the plate and take a crack at bat. You get to hoot and holler from your seat as a collective group, and even for the total newbie, taking in a **Mariners game** makes for a pretty fun day.

But going on a group date with the other forty-eight thousand folks in the stadium can be daunting, so do a little preplanning to skip the stress and make the evening a home run (see what we did there?). Rather than deal with the parking headache of driving down to T-Mobile Park, consider starting your evening back in the ID at **ChuMinh Tofu and Vegan Deli**. Try any one of their vegan banh mi on crispy, then squishy, French baguettes loaded up with spicy proteins, herbs, veggies, and a sweet-and-sour radish spectacular. Even solid meat-eaters have been charmed by these hefty sandwiches. Take them and trek the fifteen-ish-minute walk down to T-Mobile Park, where you're allowed to bring in outside food in single servings, so you can scarf down the deliciousness while shouting quotes from *A League of Their Own*.

This trick works for other games, too. Eat in the ID, and then walk over to the stadium. In this case, to watch some of the greatest soccer players on earth, the **OL Reign** at Lumen Field. Even if a game or match feels like a foreign language class you slept through in college, you are no doubt aware of Megan Rapinoe, the purple-haired phenom who was named one of *Time*'s 100 Most Influential People of 2020 for her activism, awe-inspiring athleticism, and OL Reign superstardom.

CELEBRATE HAPPINESS

Two rules apply to any and all dates in the ID: come hungry and in a festive mood. The overabundance of options can be overwhelming, but we've got you. Try beginning with Seattle's oldest Chinese restaurant, **Tai Tung**! Founded in 1935 by Grandpa Quan, the family-owned spot has had many faithful fans over the years (plus a documentary, and possibly some ghosts), including the one and only Bruce Lee. The fam says Lee always sat at the same back table and ordered his two faves—Oyster Sauce Beef and Garlic Shrimp—and you can do the same.

Even older than Tai Tung is **Maneki**, the city's longest-running Japanese restaurant, sharing its name with the traditional little waving cat figurine known for bringing good luck to its owner. Opened in 1904, Maneki is so beloved, it has managed to outlive two separate global pandemics a hundred years apart. See how it created a legion of superfans by slipping into one of their tatami rooms, tossing back a sake, and letting the sushi flow.

And when you're not stuffing the belly full of goodness, don't forget to play. That can be as simple as picking up panda beauty masks at **Uwajimaya** for a home spa day, or popping into **Books Kinokuniya** for a new puzzle to squirrel away for a lazy Sunday. But make it a point to stop by the lovely **Hing Hay Park**, which literally translates to "Celebrate Happiness Public Park"! The park's brick square boasts a stunning red-posted **Grand Pavilion** built in Taipei and is a wonderful spot to watch folks practicing martial arts moves, cheer on intense public table tennis games, or join the **annual celebrations for Lunar New Year or summer Dragonfest**.

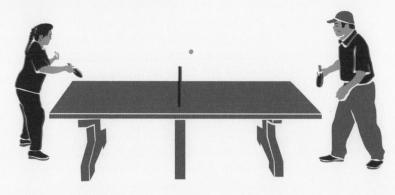

Capitol Hill • Pike • Pine • Madison • Madrona

From its welcoming rainbow crosswalks to its turn in the national spotlight, this neighborhood goes all out. Newer residents may complain about the hubbub, but Capitol Hill is, and will always be, loud and proud. If you're looking for the kind of night that goes on 'til morning, this is the place for that. And if you find yourself in need of a quiet morning that leads into a lazy afternoon, it's there for you too.

TROPICAL PUNCH

In the depths of Seattle's gray haze of winter, there are two options for survival: book a trip to Hawaii or try this tropical-inspired date. (One is going to cost you a lot less.) Begin with the absolute glory of the **Volunteer Park Conservatory**. Originally proposed in 1893, it took until 1912 to complete the Victorian-style greenhouse modeled on London's Crystal Palace with 3,426 glass panes painstakingly placed into its framework.

Inside the always toasty and humid haven, you'll find five houses of flora on display: fern, palms, succulents, bromeliads, and a seasonal potpourri. Saunter through each, taking in the brilliant colors of pineapple-cousin bromeliad, the spikiest of cacti, or even a little *Jurassic Park* cosplay in the fern section. It all feels good.

Keep the warm vibes going with a secret drink at **Inside Passage**. To get to this tropical-inspired speakeasy, check in with the host at Rumba as soon as possible to get guided into the hidden back bar that offers drinks so entertaining you'll quickly forget the temps outside. There's the *Goonies*-inspired One-Eyed Willy cocktail, which is a skull full of rums, vanilla, banana, and more served from a smoking treasure chest. Yes, you read all that correctly. Need even more pizzazz? Try the tequila-based flaming Dinglehopper. Winter who?

EAT, DRINK, AND BE GAY

Sometimes you need to take your date out for an extra dose of fun, and these local haunts fit the bill for their inclusivity and fabulousness. This neighborhood offers up so many good options, you can choose your own adventure. Here are three to get you started:

Queer/Bar: If you're a fan of fun and fashion, Queer/Bar should be on your drinking list. Not only are there weekly karaoke nights (Cher anyone?) and Sunday brunch, this is the house that drag built. There's live viewings of *RuPaul's Drag Race,* and the calendar is chock-full of rotating *Drag Race* alums like Valentina and Raja, as well as hometown heroine Bosco.

Pony: In the 1930s, it was a little local gas station, but in 2009, it became *the* tiny beloved gay dive. There's the sunset-facing outdoor patio and firepit for friend hangs, and a DJ-powered mini dance floor on the inside, where fellas can shake it to everything from disco to punk. And it might have one of the only glory holes left in the PNW to boot.

Wildrose: Lesbian bars are in short order in America these days. With less than two dozen left around the entire country, Seattle's been lucky to be home to the woman-owned and operated Wildrose since 1984. Known for their Taco Tuesdays and lo-fi vibes, check the calendar for DJ nights to dance your butt off.

MANUAL STIMULATION

Is there anything better than taking yourself out for a leisurely solo date after a long week? Better yet, one stuffed with rejuvenating culture and entertainment to thoroughly rev you up? Start at the literary heart of the city, **Elliott Bay Book Company**. Opened since 1973 (but in Cap Hill since 2010), the twenty-thousand-square-foot warehouse—with its exposed trusses, towering ceilings, and that special book smell—is a place for lingering aisle wanders before you select your next paperback friend. Not sure what to get? The well-read staff recommendations on the shelves are always a good place to start.

Next up, visit the ever-colorful **Museum of Museums**. With its hallmark neon sign, the mid-century building is like a nesting doll of museums with formal exhibition spaces and three additional on-site museums plus murals, rotating installations, art classes, a theater, a conceptual gift shop, and ever-changing pop-ups. The potential for what you see could be anything from a

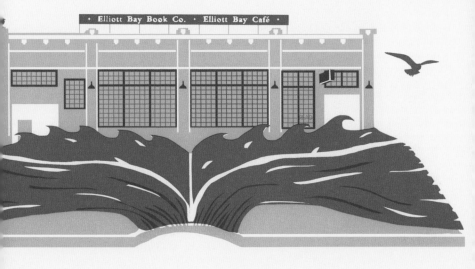

group exhibit on Afrofuturism to a magazine release party to immersive displays that'll blow your dang mind. Be open for anything and you surely won't be disappointed.

Reward yourself for being a culturephile by heading over to **Ristorante Machiavelli**. A Capitol Hill favorite for more than thirty years, known as much for its gooey eggplant parmigiana and tiramisu-like Il Diplomatico as it is for their friendly staff. They don't take reservations, so show up right when they open and try to snag a window seat for primo people watching.

Now as the evening rolls around, you've got some options depending on the calendar. Every other Wednesday, try hitting up one of the **Sorrento Hotel's Silent Reading Parties** held in their stunning Fireside Room with its famed Rookwood tiles. Here, a cross section of Seattleites gather, from famous creatives to students, to read their favorite works quietly to themselves while resident musician Paul Matthew Moore plays a pleasant live soundtrack on the piano.

In the mood for more of a silly time? Try **Central Cinema**. The second-run theater lovingly built by Kevin and Kate Spitzer features cozy couches and salvaged seats from Swedish hospital's auditorium and screens everything from kung fu flicks to old classics. And by "old classics," we mean screen gems like the truly wonderful '90s-style/music/soul patches of Cameron Crowe's *Singles* (the movie's iconic apartment building is just a few blocks away). Make sure to drop in on one of their **Movie Cat Trivia** nights, where you can indulge in fun movie trivia and cats drawn into some of your favorite film scenes.

VINYL FLING

Let the lazy day commence! Hit up **Porchlight Coffee & Records** for a morning cup of joe and, you guessed it, some leisurely flipping through vinyl. The small space belies the variety of their collection, where you can nab anything from Darlene Love and Dean Martin to Orville Peck and Childish Gambino.

Then cruise on over to the Madison Park location of **Belle Epicurean Bakery** to order up a perfect quiche Lorraine or baguette sandwich from the classical French patisserie-trained husband-and-wife team of Carolyn and Howard Ferguson. Get baked goods to go so you can picnic to your heart's content.

In the springtime, hit **Azalea Way at Washington Park Arboretum UW Botanic Gardens**. You might know the arboretum for its big, beautiful trees and heavy canopies, but come mid-April, this three-quarter-mile-long easy walk explodes in color with bright flowering azaleas, dogwoods, and cherry blossoms. Planted in 1939 by the Seattle Garden Club, these pretty babies have been witness to strolling lovers for nearly a century. Take a gander and then plunk down to devour your lunch.

Now, if it is summertime, the answer is, of course, to go "suns out, buns out" at **Madison Park**. Don your swimsuit and lay out a picnic blanket to claim your patch of the often-bumpin' four-hundred-foot beach. Not only does the neighborhood park have a bathhouse with restrooms on-site and some killer people watching, it has a floating dock where you could possibly enjoy your baguettes for a truly unique lunch experience.

U-District

If you think U-Dub and its environs are just for college students, you're missing out on some of the most romantic spots the city has to offer. From blossom-lined promenades to bayside docks to rooftop love seats, there's no shortage of places to make out like handsy teenagers.

BE KIND REWIND

Step 1: Head to Seattle's last video rental shop, **Scarecrow Video**, to comb through its massive library (more than 130,000 titles!) covering everything from your faves to rare and hard-to-find films. And we mean *rare*. As in they carry dozens and dozens of films that even the Library of Congress doesn't have copies of. There's even one dating back to 1891! Your job is for each of you to check out the film that featured your first full-blown Hollywood crush.

Step 2: Take your movies and swing by **Off the Rez** in the Burke Museum for some takeout. Here owners Mark McConnell (Blackfeet) and Cecilia Rikard use inspiration from McConnell's childhood to serve fry bread recipes loaded with savory ingredients or a perfect lemon curd. Order all the things and grab your bags to go.

Step 3: Pull out the projector or fire up the laptop, and snuggle on in and get ready to share that first true love with your partner. Spill all the embarrassing crush details—when you realized it, how it manifested, what it felt like inside when their faces lit up the screen.

One hypothetical example would be chomping on fry bread as you detail out the intense battle that raged in your soul between Jason Priestley's and Luke Perry's eyebrows before you finally settled on Perry's due to the cute little scar he has on the right one, and then you watch the film version of *Buffy the Vampire Slayer*, where Perry *also* slays? Oh, not for you? What about chowing the quinoa salad before a joint discussion about the importance of Dolly Parton to the world and a screening of *Best Little Whorehouse in Texas* where she shows up Burt Reynolds in every scene while wearing lingerie? Again, these are just *hypothetical* examples.

SUCH GREAT HEIGHTS

Two lovers gazing at the stars together definitely isn't a new idea. Odds are even our early ancestors likely had crushes with whom they stared up at the sky. But there are new and inventive ways to take in the heavens. How about a visit to the **James Turrell Skyspace** for starters? Located at the **Henry Art Gallery**, viewers enter an enclosed rotunda and can look up to see uninterrupted views of the sky. The combination of the format and the ever-changing atmosphere means each visit will look a little different every time, so it's worth returning for quiet, thoughtful gazing again and again.

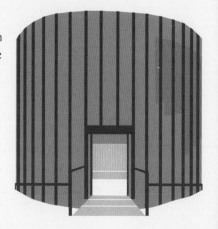

But since most dates work best with some talking, too, head to the **Mountaineering Club** after to instigate the verbal portion. Perched on the top of the **Graduate Seattle hotel**, you can check in for your reservation down in the lobby near the fancy fireplace before heading up. The vintage mountain climbing equipment is neat, and drinks named after Washington locations like the Rainier Rose (gin, rose, lemon, pineapple, salt, and tonic!) are fun, but the 360-degree views over the whole city are the real prize.

HOT TIP: Try getting a spot out on the deck on the Fourth of July for a bird's-eye view of the firework festivities without any of the neck craning.

MEZCAL FLOAT

Agua Verde Cafe & Paddle Club is the one-stop shopping of dates. The Fred Meyer of easy planning, if you will. It all begins by renting one of their kayaks (you can opt for two singles or cuddle up in a double) and then choose east or west. Going west means you can paddle to Lake Union to take in downtown views, peep Hanks's houseboat from *Sleepless in Seattle,* and look at the mishmash of old and new Seattle together. Head east to go through the Montlake Cut, the Arboretum, and Union Bay natural area, which is chock-full of frogs and turtles resting on a bounty of lily pads. You might even spot a great blue heron looking for lunch.

Speaking of lunch, the beauty of this date is the second you hit the dock, a frosty margarita and a pile of chips with guac await. While you're killing time before the Oaxacan cheese–stuffed quesadillas come out, you can post those stellar turtle pics for the world to see.

IN BLOOM—Cherry blossom trees are not native to the area, though Pacific Northwesterners all look to them as a sign of cheer after dreary days. In 1912, Tokyo mayor Yukio Ozaki donated cherry trees across the country, and eventually thirty-one of those trees ended up at the Quad at UW. Right around spring break, pay a visit to the pink explosion for a joyful walk.

CLASSIC MOVIE NIGHT—For more than fifty years, the Grand Illusion Cinema has been serving up flicks, making it the longest-running independent cinema in the city. Take yourselves out for a midweek movie night and indulge in a butter popcorn bucket and a big-screen viewing of *Xanadu, Hedwig and the Angry Inch,* or even a Marx Brothers gem.

LOUDER THAN LOVE—If your love language is adjacent to or centered on Chris Cornell, you should definitely make the trek to the *A Sound Garden* sculpture that inspired the band's name. Next to Warren G. Magnuson Park and designed by sculptor Douglas Hollis, twelve twenty-one-foot-high towers have organ pipes fastened to them that play notes when the wind blows.

Fremont • Wallingford • North Lake

This cluster of hip neighborhoods has a long history of doling out the quirk for greater Seattle. Families and cloistered homeowners have tempered the wild over the years, but with them came wholesome entertainment even the oddballs among us could get into. Welcome to the Center of the Universe. De Libertas Quirkas.

KEEP IT LIKE A SECRET

The challenge of working together against the clock in an escape room might be equivalent to six months of couple's therapy. So . . . perfect date! The mysteries that need solving at **Locurio** have earned it not only local raves but a number-ten spot from the Top Escape Room Project's Enthusiasts' Choice Awards. Oh, btw, that's top ten for the *entire world*, not just USA.

Here you can eschew some of the common super-violent escape room themes. Choose between The Vanishing Act, where you find out what's been happening to the missing assistants of the Great Noximillian (a world-renowned magician). Or you can try to find out the secret of a mysterious book collector in The Storykeeper.

Either celebrate your triumphant success or drown your sorrows at a different type of escape room, **The Backdoor at Roxy's**. An inconspicuous door in a parking lot lets you into a belly-shaped room where a slowly twirling disco ball and multiple chandeliers hang over couples and friends sipping drinks. Slip into a booth with reclaimed windows and eclectic décor all around or a table surrounded by red velvet to people watch.

KIDDING AROUND

Perhaps the hardest part of those first few dates can be finding what to talk about once you get past the "Where did you grow up?" and "Do you have any siblings?" talk. Which is why we encourage a date with some fun activities built in. Particularly ones that can naturally surface funny childhood stories. Which is why we say take them to see the Rubber Chicken Museum at **Archie McPhee**.

The "museum" is really a glass case located inside the entertaining novelty store. They claim to have both the world's largest rubber chicken and the world's smallest rubber chicken. All this is ridiculous, for sure, but it's the perfect segue to talk about what thing has made you laugh the hardest in your life, which will tell you a lot about a potential suitor. Then you can wander the aisles of the shop looking at tiny hands to put on a cat's paw, yodeling pickles, or cowgirl Band-Aids. You know, just the essentials.

Grab dinner around the corner at old haunt **Bizzarro Italian Cafe**. With mismatched chandeliers, bicycles swinging from the ceiling, a model airplane, and an upside-down lighted Christmas tree, it definitely skews more "child at heart" than upscale chichi. Clink goblets of wine while chomping arancini and house-made pappardelle pasta while you talk best childhood Halloween costume.

Finish the night off at **Add-a-Ball** arcade! It's a cross between the pinball arcades of your youth and a dive bar, so basically the fun of childhood without any actual children around. Explain your *Pac-Man* strategies! Scream at the Bad Cats pinball game when your ball hits the sweet spot! Play some Jenga! Just make sure to pack some hand sani in your bag, because a lotta fingers touching those buttons.

DOG DAY AFTERNOON

You ever see those happy-looking couples walking an adorable pup and feel the sharp pangs of jealousy deep down in your core? Totally normal! And good news, you can do something about it. Obviously, the easiest answer is to adopt the furball of your dreams and live inside a buddy comedy all the rest of your days, but because of mean landlords, traveling work schedules, or just uncertainty about having a tiny nonstop tooter in your home, it's not always feasible. But you can live the fantasy and help make a dog's day by signing up for a foster date with **Resilient Hearts Animal Sanctuary**. The nonprofit wants the best for the doggies and recognizes that not everyone can fully adopt, so they offer an untraditional foster program where you can literally take a little puppy or a sweet senior dog out for a single afternoon so you both can get serotonin boosts. And you and your honey can see how being a pet parent feels.

Take your new four-legged bestie down to Canal Street to pop into **Imperfetta**. The adorable little wine shop is a great place to grab an organic bottle of yum as well as to load up on some snacks for a picnic. Pick up some cheeses and mini baguettes, herb dips and little salads, shortbreads and chocolate, and anything else that sparks joy. You can also rent a game of bocce ball and a blanket to make this the easiest picnic of all time.

Post snacks, take the pooch on a leisurely stroll along the **Burke-Gilman Trail** (right outside Imperfetta) to **Gas Works Park**. You probably already know the nineteen-acre park that was once the Seattle Gas Light Company gasification plant, but have you ever gone there with the sole intent of taking a cute doggy to see other cute doggies? It'll change your life.

A GREEN FALL

Sure, you know **Green Lake** is *the* spot for summertime shenanigans, like getting a sunburn out on the floating dock. But the fun extends beyond reapplying sunscreen! Take, for example, the annual **Seafair Milk Carton Derby**, where dedicated citizens make wild floating concoctions in the shapes of dinosaurs and swans to race on the lake. Does a date get any better than this? We should point out Seafair's long history of wild entertainment like the Seafair Pirates, a select group of scallywags representing the city since 1949. Our favorite era has to be the 1970s pirates, who resemble a bell-bottomed mash-up of Captain Kangaroo and Jack Sparrow.

Then there is the long gone, glorious Green Lake Aqua Theater. It was a five-thousand-person theater with a stage, floating orchestra pit, and high-dive platforms on either side. Built in 1950 as part of Seafair, guests came to watch Swimusicals that somehow incorporated beautiful maidens doing aqua ballet along with stage dancing and comedians. Can you imagine rolling up to this without reading the event description? What a time to be alive! But because we cannot have nice things, it soon fell into disrepair. What was once stage right is now the pedestrian pier. Only the bleachers survive.

Now that we've talked past, let's talk present. Hit the fun summer things, for sure, but give Green Lake a go for a romantic fall date. The trees are crimson and golden, and sweater weather is a sexy time of year. Walk the path as maple leaves drop around you and consider going full Nicholas Sparks movie (when it's still in the happy bit) by renting a rowboat from **Greenlake Boathouse** and taking a peaceful paddle around the ducks. Finish the day off by more sweater action (this time, it's cute dogs wearing them) at the pup-friendly **Sully's Snowgoose Saloon**. It looks like a mini chalet on the outside, and inside this gem—one of six bars to initially get a liquor license at the end of Prohibition—it feels like a cozy ski cabin. Have a beer and play some cribbage by the fire. Fall will feel just fine.

GOOD TIMES, GREAT OLDIES

There's newfangled, and there's oldfangled. And sometimes you're just in the mood for the classics. For instance, breakfast at **Roxy's Diner**. It's an institution with hand-painted murals and '70s patterns that set the scene for your

traditional diner fare. Order up a giant bagel loaded up with eggs and cheese, or perhaps a latke sandwich the size of your head is more your jam? Either way, wash it all down with an ever-flowing cup of coffee while the Rolling Stones play and time comes to a standstill.

Then hit the **Fremont Sunday Market** on Thirty-Fourth Street for a helluva browse. You might already be familiar with this neighborhood mainstay for its booths of flowers, turquoise rings, or locally harvested beeswax candles. But there's a pop-up within the weekly pop-up! Step into the **Hyper Market** to snag original *Beverly Hills, 90210* collector cards, gold thingamajigs to hang your keys on, vintage tees, and attractive people rifling through it all in a parking garage turned flea market stall.

Finally, while you're in the area (and still walking off those latkes), stroll through the **Fremont Vintage Mall** to scope out mid-century furniture, bronze naked ladies, and oodles of vintage clothing. Seventies vintage tux? Flowy floral caftan? Give it a try and have some fun spinning for each other like you're Julia Roberts in a shopping montage. Don't be afraid to shell out for a WOWZA ensemble for a future event. Duos that show up looking fly AF are welcome additions to any and all parties.

HOT TIP: Every year when summer solstice rolls around, so does the Mardi Gras–style Fremont Solstice Parade. It's a trip. See giant puppets next to parade floats and dancing troupes swirling colorful capes, not to mention the famous crowd of painted naked bike riders that crash the event every year.

More Fun

TOO BRIGHT—Nights can get especially dark up in these parts. Colorful lights help. Celebrate the autumnal equinox with **Luminata**, a lantern parade around Green Lake that culminates in an illuminated art exhibition. And later in the year, **WildLanterns** takes over the Woodland Park Zoo with giant, glowing representations of wildlife and wild places.

"GREEN" LAKE—While not technically dockside, woman- and minority-owned **Dockside Cannabis** is the closest dispensary to Green Lake. Grab provisions here and get lost on the 2.8-mile path around the lake. You haven't heard Canadian geese honking until you've heard them on some old-school Kush.

WHAT'S COOKIN', GOOD LOOKIN'?—There are few things sexier than the kitchen dance. Whet your whistle with some foreplay at **Book Larder**, one of only a handful of cookbook stores in the nation. Once you've decided on a swoon-worthy recipe to prepare, head home to seal the meal.

WESTWARD, HO!—The resort-like layout of waterfront mainstay **Westward** invites you to recline into the lap of luxury. Sip bubbles and slurp oysters while seaplanes zip and dip over Lake Union. Sunny days are rightfully mobbed, but it's equally nice to bundle up and curl up with a crush by the firepit.

TURKISH DELIGHT—While not as cozy as its original spot, the riot of color and lively chatter that greet you when you enter **Café Turko** will still fill your soul with joy. Fill your stomach, too, with aromatic dishes, fried cheese, homemade ayran, and owner Süreyya Gökeri's "No Guilt" baklava.

Ballard

There's no better way to blow an afternoon than by strolling the tree-lined streets of Ballard, popping into shops, and pausing for any number of libations while people judging/watching. And while weekend nights can be a bit of a cluster, you'd be remiss to skip the nightlife on tap. Warmer months have us jockeying for grassy knolls and waterfront tables at which to soak up the rays. But really, no matter the season, Ballard's where you'll find the beating heart of Seattle.

THE BIRDS AND THE ~~BEES~~ FISH

Grab fish-and-chips to go from the locally loved **Lockspot Cafe**, which has doled out seafood to neighborhood visitors for the last century. Take your grub mere feet away into the **Carl S. English Jr. Botanical Garden**, part of the **Ballard (Hiram M. Chittenden) Locks**. Dive into your greasy fare while sitting on the terraced greens with other couples stretched out in the sun squirting sunscreen onto belly buttons or reading *actual* newspapers. While you're lounging, you'll likely notice some other fish chompers—the large colony of great blue herons across the locks at the Kiwanis Ravine. They typically arrive in February to begin their courtship routines, snag a mate, and start building out nests. Each one of these hot new couples usually produces two or three hatchlings, and you might see as many as sixty nests up in the trees. They'll dive and swoop at an intense pace (around thirty-five miles per hour!), and watching them come and go

is like a live *Nat Geo* show. You'll have to do your own David Attenborough narrations, however.

You can get a little closer to the bird party by walking across the locks, the busiest in the country. Boats as big as a Richie Rich yacht to the humble kayak can enter the lock to be raised or lowered two dozen feet to traverse between the Puget Sound and Lake Union. Walk through and daydream about what boat you'll call your own in the future and take a minute to check out the Chinook salmon using the fish ladder to swim upstream.

BAY WATCH

Plan A requires you to make friends with someone who is a member at the **Elks Lodge #827**. The Elks, like all organizations founded exclusively by men, have some raised-eyebrow-inducing history. But they now rightfully grant memberships to women, and the clubhouse is seriously fun. Located on Point Shilshole, the current lodge was built in 1978, and those vibes infuse the place with a laid-back atmosphere. The first floor has a fab waterfront terrace beach bar with drinks going for a song. You just need an invite.

Plan B requires no special handshake, is just a few feet away, and also has an amazing view for waterfront drinks. We're talking about **Ray's Café**, the upstairs casual option to Ray's Boathouse with a great patio for sipping icy drinks, counting seagulls, and sharing snacks. They don't take reservations, so think about going between peak hours or have a good long story to entertain your date while you wait for a table.

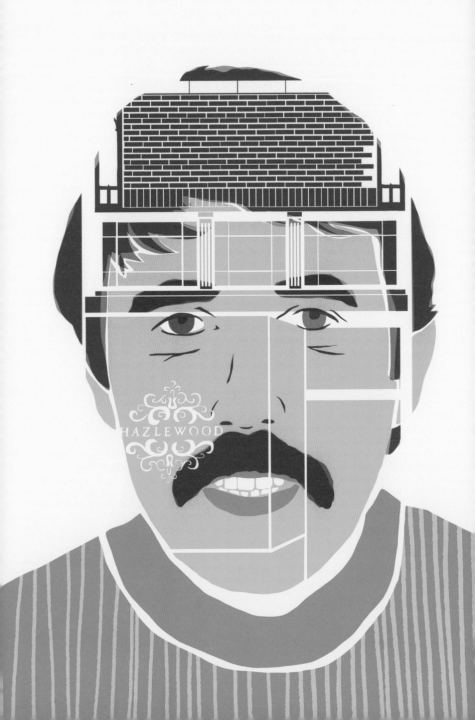

BAR-CROSSED LOVERS

Ballard the city ceased to exist on May 29, 1907, when the city's residents offi-cially voted to become part of Seattle (some say due to an *incident* involving a dead horse in Ballard's water supply). Bye, Ballard the city, hello to the bangin' Ballard neighborhood! It's an ideal place to meet for a bar crawl as a twosome or on a double date.

Mosey to the ever-moody **Hazlewood**, known for its taste in tunes (if you don't know Lee Hazlewood, that's some great date music right there), the legendary hot toddy wearing a googly-eyed sweater cozy, and some of the best people watching in the neighborhood. Slip up to the second floor to get close and get a bird's-eye view of the crowd.

We've done moody, and now hat tip to nostalgia. **Hattie's Hat** has been slinging drinks and serving up the basic bar fare your heart desires since Teddy Roosevelt was president. It's a mishmash of all the levels of sensory comfort you could ever want. It somehow has excellent cat art (including one playing a fiddle) next to the antique ornate bar along with spinning a disco ball, and it feels like you're in your parents' basement rec room again . . . in a good way. Load up on nachos, have a Bloody Mary for dinner. At Hattie's Hat, what feels good is the thing to do.

After all that, say goodbye to the evening with a final stop at **Pie Bar**, where tipsy couples sway outside the wood-paneled walls clamoring for slices of cremini mushroom or tart cherry (which is also a good nickname for your date).

MAGIC YOUR GATHERING

If wizardry, Harry Potter, that little worm guy from *Labyrinth*, Tim Curry's horned red devil, the sword fighting in *Willow*, or Falkor the Luck Dragon are your kinda thing, feels like you might be entertained by this date too. Load up crystals of all kinds at **Ballyhoo Curiosity Shop**. There's rose quartz, said to help with both self-love and fostering love for others, calcite chunks for calming the mind and bringing clarity, and pyrite nuggets (aka fool's gold) which is just gosh darn pretty! Then pop over to **Lucca** for colorful candles, earthy soaps, and a gorgeous tarot deck. Who knows, you might even pull The Lovers card.

This is not the end of your fun by a long shot. Next up? Grab a meal and a board game a block away at **Mox Boarding House**. In a rare combo, this spot has a wide-ranging menu of spinach salads, oven-baked mac and cheese, and twice-baked potatoes. It's also a fully stocked game store with tabletop games, role-playing games, and more. You can try out a huge number of games for free from their library while you eat, and if you love it, buy a copy to take home and play again later.

SMOKIN' HOT

Golden hour outdoes itself at **Golden Gardens Park**. When the sun begins its nightly melt into the horizon, the big ol' beachfront park lights up in hues of pinks and oranges for possibly the perfect backdrop for a passionate kiss. Build up to that moment by going in the afternoon with a picnic blanket and mini cooler of kombucha. Or level up by bringing your own hammock to tie up in the shady grove by the lagoon (a great spot for those in the Sunburn Instantly camp). It's fun to watch the volleyballers play and see if any boys are channeling shirtless Iceman and Maverick *Top Gun* sexy tension vibes. Sailboats lazily drift across your view, and it's a reminder that the world at sunset is grand.

Once the giant star has completed its nightly bow, take over one of the designated pits and get those coals a' cooking. Did you know that bringing the makings for s'mores to a beach bonfire is a love language unto itself? All that's left to do is eat your smushy, melty treats and cuddle.

leasure Meadows

ROM LAST week's visit to the "infernal" mills of Ballard, this week we follow the same Ballardian photographer James

Just North

While things might get a little more relaxed the farther north you venture, don't sleep on all this region has to offer. A break from the hustle and bustle will do you good. And if you *really* want to get away from it all, Edmonds presents an opportunity to spend some quiet time under the sea. Sebastian, that's your cue . . .

CARKEEKS AND GEEKS

Question: How many views do you want in a park? If the answer is *all* of them, consider a visit to **Carkeek Park**. We're talking an eyeful of the Olympic Mountains, the southern tip of Whidbey, the Puget Sound, and Kitsap Peninsula. For being just a few minutes from the city, this place is cherished for its ability to feel like another world.

Dive into the six miles of trails for a tour through ecosystems. Beyond the lovely dense forest trails, you can also see **Piper's Orchard** (the oldest orchard in Seattle!), a wetland, and a great rocky beach. Keep a mental tally going of who spots more of the fun starfish and creepy crabs all around the shore.

One more park perk? The dozens and dozens of picnic tables. Pack that lunch, bring those playing cards, and stretch out for snacks and Uno. Dropping a reverse card is a strategic flirtation.

LITTLE MERMAIDS

When you feel like you've done all the dates in the world, it's a good time to get in the car and drive north to **Edmonds Underwater Sports** equipment rental. There the helpful staff will help you get suited up with everything you need—air tanks, breathing apparatus, wet suit, weights, and fins—so you're all set to scuba. Yes, scuba.

Then make your way to the fantastic **Edmonds Underwater Park**. For more than fifty years, this little spot of marine magic has entertained both experienced divers and newbies working their Ursula cosplay vibes. There's a restroom with an outdoor shower and diver dressing rooms on-site to suit on up before going below.

Once underwater, divers can see nearly human-size lingcod cruising around fields of plumose anemones or dino-looking cabezon defending their eggs. There are sunken ships to explore along with the octopi, urchins, and starfish all doing the same. The site is a no-take area, meaning hands off the wildlife so every underwater creature can be free to be themselves. Including you.

DOLL PARTS

What do Hollywood, California, and Everett, Washington, have in common? They are the only two places in the country you can have a customized Funko Pop! figurine made in your likeness. Those adorable little versions of Batman and Batgirl, Chewy and Spider-Man, all turned into top-heavy bobbleheads come from the **Funko Pop Headquarters**, and now you two can be the bobbleheads!

Far more than a store, the amusement park–like displays of cute little Stormtroopers and Harry and Hermione in their element are worth viewing on their own. Go the extra mile by crossing through the building's Wetmore Forest room to a factory assembly area where you can build your own Funko Pop. That means customizing skin tone! Hair! Outfits! Accessories! You name it. How often can you have mini likenesses of yourself? (Well, mini likenesses that don't require a lifetime of financial and emotional support.)

Crafting creatures is hard work, and you've got fun ahead still so refuel at **K Fresh** rice bar. This locally owned build-a-bibimbap caters to all manner of eaters—keto, carnivore, vegan, and nut-free. Start by picking your rice and protein of choice, and bling out the meal with their assortment of veggies heaped into a traditional Korean stoneware bowl. Pro, but controversial, tip: pineapple and daikon radish make everything more fun.

Immortalizing yourselves in bobblehead form and getting stuffed to the gills is a fine date unto itself. But! If it's a Friday in the peak of summer, and you still got a little lust for Hollywood in your heart, add on Everett's **Sail-in Cinema**. The only waterfront movie series in Snohomish County, the Sail-in Cinema offers free movies for all—think *Spider-Man, Encanto,* and, of course *Free Willy.* Have a sailboat? Or at least access to hot sailors with a boat? Slip into one of the guest viewing, er, slips at the North Docks adjacent to the port and listen in on a local radio frequency provided preshow. Boatless? No problem there, lay a picnic blanket down at the port's **Boxcar Park** to partake in the free flicks. Low-back chairs are allowed and layers are a must what with the breeze blowing in from the water. Once the stunning sunset finishes showing off, the movies are a go. And yes, there are concessions on-site for the requisite popcorn munching.

Out West

Sandy beaches, bustling boardwalks, unironic in-line skaters? What is this? California? Cruise over on a sunny day to join the pasty hordes shedding layers and soaking up that sweet, sweet vitamin D and you'll be picking up West Seattle's good vibrations, too. Designated fire rings on Alki Beach ensure the flames can carry on into the night. Or at least until nine thirty p.m. After that, it's up to you, Casanova.

WILD WILD WEST

Hop onto the boat at Pier 50 downtown to zip you across the water on the ten-minute **West Seattle Water Taxi**. Be sure to take mental pics of how lovely downtown's skyline looks as it recedes into the distance. Once you disembark, pop straight onto the free (!) **Water Taxi Shuttle #775** to commute you down to **Alki Beach**.

Now you're living that beach life, so chill with a book, look for kite flyers, or people watch to your heart's content. But for the fun seekers, we say rent one of the ridiculous-looking tandem Surrey bikes from **Wheel Fun Rentals** that come with a bonus shade guard to protect you from the sun while pedaling. Cruise along the beach path to peep at the **Alki Point Lighthouse** or just perfect your tandem thrusts (of the pedals, you dirty bird!).

After you're all beached out, take the shuttle back to your dock stop and follow the golden umbrellas over to **Marination Ma Kai** for some deliciousness. The Hawaiian Korean cuisine manifests in tacos galore covered in their signature spicy-sweet Nunya sauce, kimchi fried rice, and loaded luau plates. Eat outside and take in the lovely view before you ease your full, tired, sun-drunk body back onto the taxi again.

HOT TIP: In June, be sure to visit the famed Flower Houses on Alki Avenue. Nestled in between high condos, owner Randie Stone purchased the homes in 1989 and has them beautifully blinged out with flowers so enchanting it seems straight out of a fairy tale when they bloom.

EASY DOES IT

Seattle has a dearth of public outdoor pools (two, to be exact), but thanks be that **Colman Pool** is wonderful. The heated outdoor pool is salt water (good for those muscles and far less smelly than chlorine), with fifty-meter swim lanes, slides, and room for *lots* of water babies. Located in **Lincoln Park**, it

requires a bit of a walk through the park to get there, but once there, you can dive into the warm waters of a beachside pool with one of the best views of the Sound around. Of course, it is of the utmost importance to check the pool schedule for open swim times and arrive as early as humanly possible before it gets overrun. Godspeed.

Assuming you went bright and early to exercise the bod, fuel up after with a visit to **Easy Street Cafe**, the diner appendage to the hallowed **Easy Street Records**. Sidle up to a table for a mushroom-and-sweet-pepper-stuffed Woody Guthrie Farmers Omelet or maybe the Dolly Parton Stack (of pancakes). Post carb-loading, comb the aisles for some new vinyl to spin at home, or some old water-related faves (obvi Pearl Jam's "Oceans," FTW).

East Side

Snobby types have been turning their noses up at the east side since before Bill Gates was born, but those unwilling to make the trek over Lake Washington are missing out on a whole swath of what greater Seattle has to dish up. Whether it be a posh getaway or just some unbeatable cheap eats, these burbs are more bumpin' than they might let on.

GOES DOWN LIKE A FINE WINE

We firmly believe that a good date can be done on the cheap. But we also believe there are the times—big anniversaries, birthdays that end in zero, fabulous personal milestones—to go ahead and spend that money, honey. One way to plunk it down is a luxurious wine-filled weekend in Woodinville.

Book yourself two nights at **Willows Lodge**, the posh place located on a handful of acres along the Sammamish River Trail. You could easily hunker down for the duration at the resort, which boasts rooms that include two-person soaking tubs, stone fireplaces, and balconies perfect for coffee drinking and pointing out pretty birds. Then there's the relaxation pool in a Japanese-inspired courtyard and a full spa with detox wraps, deep-tissue massages, and aromatherapy facials. Or borrow a pair of bikes from the concierge and pedal around the riverside trail before having dinner in the lodge's **Fireside Lounge** or **Barking Frog** restaurant.

But let's say you do have the urge to leave the love den for a bit. There are more than one hundred wineries in the area, but given the nature of wine tasting (you know, drinking alcohol), we suggest hitting the ones within an easy walk. Try lounging out at **The Deck** at **DeLille Cellars** (in the old Redhook brewery) where you can sun and sip everything from a cucumber and Asian pear–noted Chardonnay to a round red-blend mix of Mourvèdre, Grenache, and Syrah. Also a short meander? **Novelty Hill-Januik Winery**. Acclaimed winemaker Mike Januik released his first Columbia Valley harvest back in 1984, so you could say he's been around the barrel. The winery expanded their outdoor space in 2022, meaning you can now roam both upper and lower gardens and go full Euro leisure by rolling some bocce balls.

Let's say after a long day of playing the part of Dionysus, you want a break from wine. It could happen. Try paying a visit to **21 Acres Farm Market**, a climate-focused market selling local produce from area farms that is all sustainably grown and pesticide-free; the market is surrounded by lovely scenery, including a summer wildflower field. The deli offerings are legit and full of food from the area, like hummus veggie wraps with Woodinville-grown lettuce and roasted leek scapes or pasta salads with local mozzarella and French breakfast radishes.

Before you pack up for the weekend, make the time (and liver space) to pop into **Woodinville Whiskey Co.** for an affordable tasting flight that includes ninety-proof port cask-finished bourbon whiskey, a rye whiskey, and even a barrel-aged maple syrup! Make a reservation in advance for a distillery tour if the mechanical stirring of golden booze is a personal turn-on. Post-tasting, inch next door to the **Hollywood Tavern**. In the area since the 1940s, this place gives you all the things you want in a country roadhouse: lawn games, a firepit, deep-fried pickles, and chocolate–peanut butter milkshakes.

FOR OLD TIME'S SAKE

Looking for a nice little day trip to sharpen your hunting skills? Try heading to **Snohomish for antiquing**—truly the more imaginative version of The Most Dangerous Game. There are dozens and dozens of stores in the area offering everything from cheapie egg cups to ornate, high-end furniture. Start by meandering **First Street**, where the window shopping is good but the diving in is even better. Get lost combing through shelves of mid-century crackle glass vases in all colors of the rainbow, delicate gold-rimmed flower teacups, or even phones from before they were smart. It's worth noting owners of antique stores sometimes have a reputation for being cantankerous, especially when they think you might touch (and possibly break) something, so take care maneuvering through the aisles.

If you're ready for some history, this time of the potentially haunted variety, pay a visit to the **Oxford Saloon**. Built in 1900, it's had various business incarnations over the years, ranging from dry goods store to brothel to saloon. And in some of those dealings, violence was a regular occurrence (more likely during the brothel and saloon eras, rather than fisticuffs over the selling of flour and buttons, but perhaps things got

spicy in the mercantile). One creeper ghost you might want to keep an eye out for is Henry. Henry was a cop who hung around the saloon a lot and was killed when a bar brawl turned into a knife fight. He shows up the most in the women's bathroom, where many have reported not only seeing him but *being pinched by him*. Whatttt?

Now that you have the important facts, you can choose whether or not to order a drink with your jalapeño poppers or opt for dehydration to avoid Ol' Henry. But if you're there in the evening, stick around for one of their live shows, which can include everything from acoustic jams to an Elvis tribute band.

TASTING MENU

You know that thing when you've been dating awhile and one person says, "What should we do for dinner tonight?" and the other stares blankly in response? This is the cure for that, namely, a trip to Bellevue's Bel-Red neighborhood where a mile-long strip of Asian restaurants await to fill your bellies gloriously full. Sit underneath the collage of glowing neon signs at **Spicy PoPo** for a dragon-adorned bowl with sizzling Szechuan Fish or load up on Taiwanese pickled cucumber and sautéed green bean sprouts from **MonGa Café**. Or maybe you wanna chomp into some chewy, delicious dumplings (a definitive cure for work stress)? Try the Xiao Long Bao at **Supreme Dumplings**. Ooooh, and don't forget about the crunch taro patties at **Sukhothai Restaurant**. Heck, just zoom around your map app and form a progressive plan for appetizers, entrées, and dessert at any place that entices you with their menu. Before you head out, stop into the **Asian Family Market** for a bubble tea (if you've got room), and pick up the ingredients to re-create the favorite thing you just ate.

Down South

A destination for fun since 1869, when a local saloon and brothel keeper created the region's first horse track in Georgetown, the area was also host to the Northwest's first automobile races as well as the first demonstrations of flight. One-hundred-some-odd years later, thrill seekers can partake in airplane-less skydiving and karaoke in decommissioned train cars. Talk about progress!

YOU LOOK GEORGEOUS

If you love shopping *and* vintage trailers, boy, have we got the date for you. Saunter from cute little shop to shop while browsing at the **Georgetown Trailer Park Mall**, where each trailer requires you to duck your head (literally) before you can scope out its wares. There's one-of-a-kind mesh fashion designs to custom aquariums to an actual adorable shotgun wedding chapel made from a shipping container. There's only room for two pews, but it includes a good story to tell your friends.

Already ready for a break? Why not? The delightful back patio at **Fonda La Catrina** is a good spot to sit, sip an icy horchata, and munch a quesadilla while gearing up for the next step of the date.

Refreshed, pay a visit to **Fantagraphics Bookstore & Gallery**. Since the 1970s, this press has published beloved comic books, graphic novels, and manga to kazillions of adoring fans. At their storefront, everything currently in print is for sale, and, bonus, you can also see their erotic Eros Comix imprint. Oh la la! Moreover, they have a **Damaged Room** with super-slashed prices on beat-up, out-of-print, and often unavailable books.

Not only is this a fun stop, it also happens to share a space with **Georgetown Records**, where the two often host events together like art shows, book signings, and other merrymaking. The record shop has all the usuals, from Bowie to *Kind of Blue*, in addition to a great world music collection with an Armenian Turkish section backed up behind the Hawaiian and Mexican traditional tunes. Buy them all for good house vibes.

SPARKS ARE FLYING

For those of us who grew up in the *Point Break* era (Did you know a PNW beach dubbed in for Australia in the iconic final scene?), we are aware that the concept of skydiving is sexy. Tight jumpsuits! Adrenaline! Graceful air dancing! "Bodhi, I am an FBI agent!" However, there are a multitude of reasons why one might not want to fling themselves out of a perfectly good airplane. Enter **iFly** indoor skydiving.

Located in Tukwila, couples helmet up, don their flight suits, and then hop into the recirculating wind tunnel. There, four massive fans in perfectly placed locations create airflow in a loop that's directed into a flying chamber, where it becomes strong enough to pick up a human and simulate skydiving. No planes needed. Just choose who wants to be Keanu and who wants to be Swayze.

GARDEN OF STONE

Brunch and a garden? We know, we know—obvious yes, basic no. While this date idea isn't new, you could conceivably go on Sunday brunch and garden dates to different places every weekend and have an absolutely delightful new experience each time.

So go ahead and give that brunch life a go at **The Stonehouse Cafe** on Rainier Avenue South. In the 1920s, this was a little gas station, and became a neighborhood icon for its distinct appearance—it looks like a witch's house with its stacked stone architecture. In 2015, it became a cafe that boasts a water view directly across the street from Lake Washington with *all-day breakfast*. Because sometimes you just want hot, cinnamon-y, syrupy French toast, you know?

After brunch, it's a five-minute drive to **Kubota Garden**, a beautiful twenty-acre Japanese garden. Started in 1927 by self-taught gardener and Japanese immigrant Fujitaro Kubota, it was originally a mud-pit blank slate before he set about building a gathering space for the city's growing Japanese community. In his lifetime, he saw it become a cultural center for the community before he was forcibly removed from it for four years during World War II when he and his family were placed in an internment camp. When they were finally allowed back to their homes, he rebuilt

it. When he was ninety-three, the Japanese government gave him Fifth Class Order of the Sacred Treasure, "for his achievements in his adopted country, for introducing and building respect for Japanese Gardening in this area." As you walk through his life's work of beautiful footbridges, multiple ponds, shimmery koi swimming, and trees that turn a stunning gold in autumn, you can't help but feel the love he put into this place. If this isn't a good date spot, we don't know what is.

EXPRESS YOURSELF

Question: Have you ever been inside a Chinese restaurant that is also a series of decommissioned train cars, one used by President Franklin D. Roosevelt as he traveled the country on his 1944 reelection campaign? Oh, you haven't? Consider a visit, then, to SoDo's **Orient Express**. The quick facts: the opinions on the food vary widely, but the unusual atmosphere always impresses (as do its famed stiff drinks). Bring a gaggle of friends and hit the lit (literally and figuratively) karaoke train for a night of spring rolls and singing.

SOUL MATES

A day date option commences with a suggestion. Get up early and get in a morning visit to **Seward Park**, a work in progress for decades. There was the initial proposal in 1892, then the bathhouse was added in the '20s, and in the '50s the city carved a Greek amphitheater out of the south hillside, where there was spiffy orchestral and dance productions for ages. What we're saying is this place already has great date karma. Plus, add on all the activities on the three-hundred-acre site like "I Spying" loads of eagles nests, chasing each other on the miles of bike trails, and stretching out on the many beaches that line the peninsula.

After a full morning of chilling at the waterfront, now is the time to hit **Geraldine's Counter** (they close at three p.m.!). The Columbia City spot regularly has a line for brunch, so we say go get an herb omelet after noon. Fingers crossed that the line has dissipated and you've worked up the appetite to add a side of fries just because.

Now as far as an evening option in the area, might we suggest calling upon **Island Soul Rum Bar & Soul Shack**. For more than fifteen years, owner Theo Martin has served up his fusion of Caribbean cuisine meets Louisiana bayou soul food to hordes of local fans. Wash it all down with traditional companion cocktails like a dark and stormy with house-made ginger beer. Delish!

Then journey over to **The Royal Room** for a show. The cozy venue is more jazz club than concert venue, which is perfect for a sweet night together. Befittingly, their calendar has a ton of great jazz options, but there's also salsa bands, swing nights, and even a monthly "Men Aren't Funny" showcase of women and nonbinary comedians sticking it to the patriarchy. What's not to love?

ZONE 3
A Short Drive Away

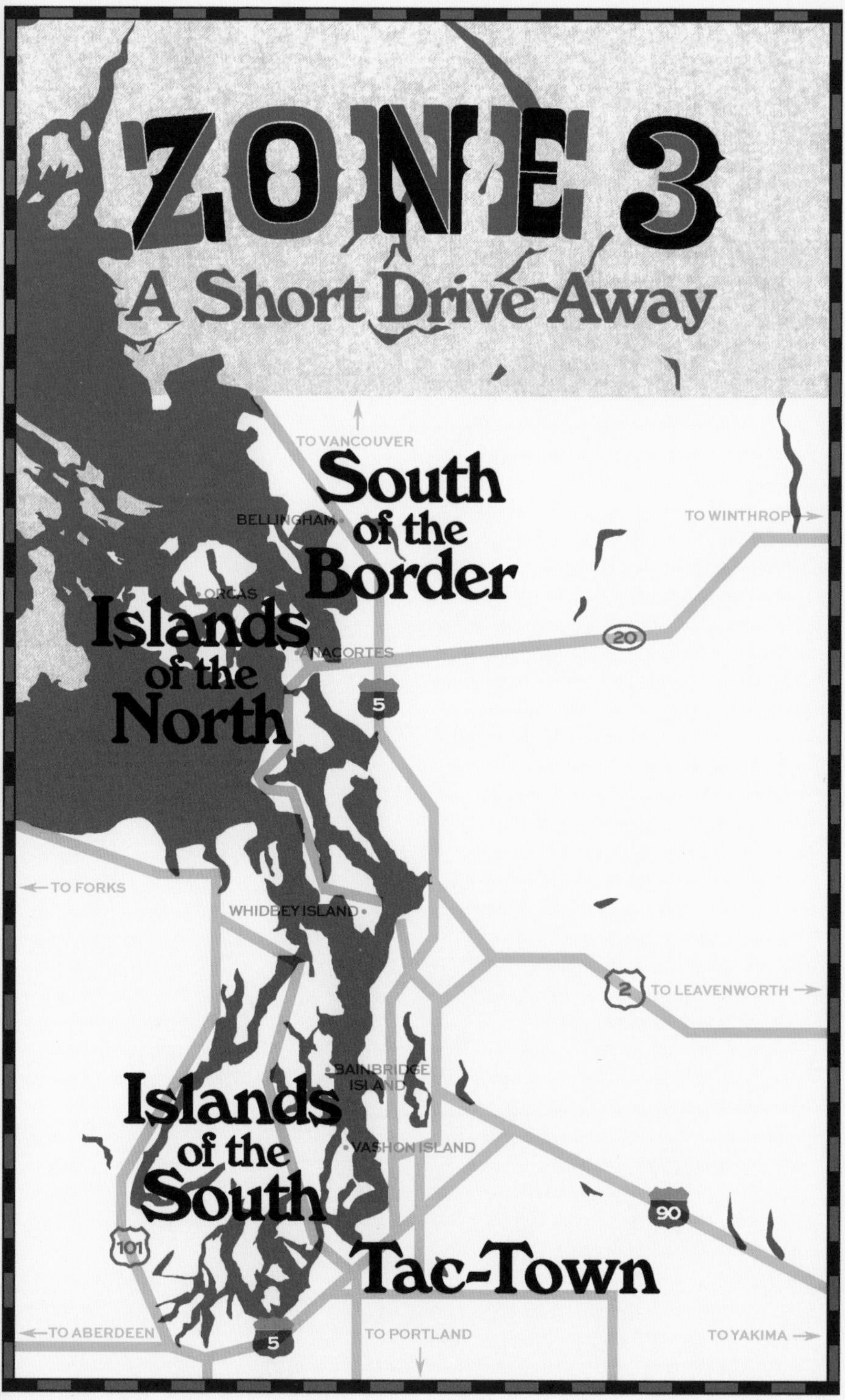

Tac-Town

Sure, there are a plenty of places to sneak away for an overnighter, but they don't call this place the City of Destiny for nothing. Hidden gems abound for those willing to brave the southbound traffic. Spend a weekend exploring the quaint alleyways and expansive greenspaces, and you might just spend the weeks after scrolling through real estate apps and questioning your life choices. It is your destiny.

TEMPLE OF THE ~~DOG~~ ELK

Weekend in Tacoma? The easiest home base of all lies in the multi-optioned **McMenamins Elks Temple** with hotel rooms on the upper floors and restaurants and entertainment a plenty below. Built during World War I, when for some reason fraternal organizations were thriving, the Elks crafted this massive downtown clubhouse complete with the **Spanish Ballroom**. Built so couples could strut their stuff on the dance floor, a hundred years later, it's still doing that as a venue for everything from '80s dance nights to ABBA tribute bands to PNW bands like Horse Feathers.

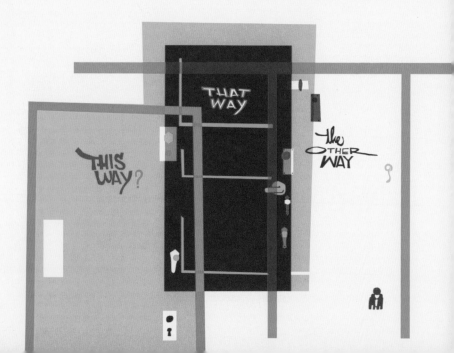

Sweetest ...

Six months ago ...
now my heart was
empty.

Then you came into my
life.

And now ...
like a burst of ... and
love. I can't wait for
more months with my ...

Hey,

You looking
real good over there
I meant just ...
... you
mine forever

Life ... moments!
I have ... of my life sitting
across from me. She is everything
to me.
Jay 1/18/19

HARBOR

CL

Whether or not you're there for a show, there's a lot to keep you entertained on-site. Try besting each other at a round of pool in **Doc's Bar**, or downing some egg rolls and a mai tai at the tropical-vibed **Old Hangout** bar that has an indoor waterfall and regular faux lightning storms. For those that love a little mystery, you must go on a quest to discover **The Vault**. It's a secret bar none of the staff will help you find, which makes the cold cocktail upon arrival all the sweeter. Sip it while watching through little glass squares as clueless passersby walk overhead. (And that's the only hint we're gonna give you.)

But let's say you actually want to leave your hotel for a bit. Fair! Try a stroll down the neighboring **Opera Alley**. Once the spot where Tacomans gathered post opera, now it's a cute little alleyway with vibrant murals and dimly lit places perfect for dates. For dinner try **Over the Moon Cafe**. The little brick restaurant was once the backstage of the city's first opera house, but for the last twenty years, it's been serving up northwest cuisine from scratch. While waiting for your food, open the little box on your table—past guests leave love notes you can read aloud to each other for inspiration, or gift your own sonnet to the box.

But, hold up, we're not done with secret bars yet. Directly across the alley from the cafe, you'll notice a wooden helm (a.k.a a ship's steering wheel)

LIGHTS

OYSTERS   HALIBUT   CRAB LEGS

hanging above a doorway. That's your cue to enter the unmarked door to the left to be transported to the sea at **Devil's Reef** bar. This bar has everything: bamboo booths, fishnets, mood lighting that looks like its reflecting off water, and rum drinks *that glow*. If you can get a table, this is the place to spill some secrets.

As far as activities that don't involve imbibing, be sure to check if your visit coincides with one of the **Tacoma Vintage Walks** (held every last Saturday of the month) at the historic Union Club. The pop-up vintage marketplace described as "like an art walk for vintage lovers" boasts more than a dozen vintage sellers selling clothing, macramé plant hangers, and knickknacks.

WHAM BAM
THANK YOU CLAM

Just a couple of blocks from the Elks Temple, we say have a waterfront day of fun. Grab one of the city's Razor electric scooters and start zooming your butt down the lovely **waterfront path on Ruston Way**. The childhood glee that comes with scootin' is date enough in itself, but the path provides many an entertaining stop along the way. One of the first things you'll come across is the **Fuzhou Ting**, a beautiful pavilion in a Chinese-style garden donated by Tacoma's sister city, Fuzhou, China, and is definitely worth a photo stop. (Plus, you might spot a wedding in progress!)

Keep on trucking and soon you'll see the twinkling sign of **Harbor Lights**. For more than fifty years, this waterfront restaurant overlooking Commencement Bay has kept Tacomans and its visitors stuffed. Literally. They are perhaps most known for their giant portions of seafood, including a ginormous bucket of clams. Our recommendation is to share anything if you want to be able to keep on rolling.

Next on the list (if it's a summer weekend, that is), hit the lovely **Point Ruston Farmers Market**. Open every Sunday from June to September, it's a fantastic lazy wander. Buy up some fresh produce to snack on or delightful local pickles for your next pickle party, sauces for your next sauce party, or cabbage for your next cabbage party—or just sit and watch the kids and dogs play in the adjacent splash pad of the Grand Plaza.

THAT'S A GOOD POINT

Make a whole day of it at **Point Defiance Park**, one of the largest in the area. Though you can ignore the persistent rumor it is the second largest in the country, because Portland's Forest Park and San Francisco's Golden Gate Park both beat it as far as square acres. It might not be the biggest, but it is jam-packed with a ton of activities, and you can make this date match any budget by going fully free to splashing cash about.

Within the 760-acre park, the options abound, and it's best to use the time of year as your guide when honing in on your plan of action. In the fall, walk the paths through the old-growth forest and notice the changing leaves and other signs of autumn rolling on in. Or take a cliffside hike, stopping frequently to take in the many views of Dalco Passage or Vashon Island. In the spring, saunter through the many gardens on-site looking for the rhododendrons, fuchsias, and iris all starting to show off their allure. Or stop by the **off-leash dog park** to watch fur balls running with perma smiles on their faces. In the winter, bundle up and hit **Fort Nisqually** inside the park to see what life was like on the Puget Sound back in 1855. Originally an outpost for the Hudson Bay company, it's now a museum. Before you go, take a listen to the podcast Fort Nisqually Living History Museum put out in 2021 that brought in representatives from the Muckleshoot, Nisqually, Puyallup,

723

Steilacoom, and Squaxin Island tribes to talk about how the Puget Sound Treaty War affected the Indigenous communities.

And then, of course, there's summer. When that magic comes around, best to block out the whole day. Pop into the **Dahlia Trial Garden** to see giant poky blooms grown from tubers sent from dahlia growers as far as New Zealand and England. Now that the sunny flower walk has you footloose and full of fancy, get out on the water.

At the **Point Defiance Marina**, sign all the waivers and take a fourteen-foot boat with a little trolling motor and head out. With hourly rates starting at fifty dollars (which includes safety gear and gas), you can take a coastal cruise just for the views, or you can extend your rental long enough to jet up to Gig Harbor and dock the boat outside **Tides Tavern**. Sit out on the deck, shoot back an oyster, devour one of their giant salads, and sip a cold drink like the baller you are. But make sure to have the boat back on time because even Cinderella's carriage turned into a pumpkin when she was late.

More Fun

ALMA LOVE—
The Spanish Ballroom
definitely isn't the only
place in town to catch a show.
See what the cool kids are doing
at **Alma**. The five-hundred-capacity
venue is also a recording studio that has
both a patio and rooftop restaurant. Their
calendar is wide-ranging, with Native art markets
and drag shows to punk rock flea markets and singer/song-
writer performances.

JIVE DIVE—Speaking of music, if you have a deep love of anecdotes, pay a visit to the concrete coffeepot known as **Bob's Java Jive**. Within these storied walls, Nirvana played, Neko Case bartended, and monkeys once ran amok. Have a drink and see what other tidbits you might pick up from this cultural landmark.

OLD HAUNT—The story of **Thornewood Castle** begins five hundred years ago when the English castle was first constructed. Then one hundred years ago, Chester Thorne had the manor shipped to Lakewood and reconstructed into a stunning twenty-seven-thousand-square-foot Gothic Tudor wonder. Now, depending on who you ask, this stunning historic hotel makes an ideal wedding venue or is a hotbed of paranormal activity, with regular ghost sightings of *all* members of the Thorne family and even a full-fledged phantom cocktail party. Or maybe both?

ROM-COM ME—In 1999, the world was given a gift in the form of *10 Things I Hate About You*. Not only is the high school pop culture version of *Taming of the Shew* an absolute time capsule, it was our introduction to Heath Ledger. Filmed in part at Tacoma's storied **Stadium High School** (built in 1891 to be a French-château-inspired luxury hotel), cruise on by and sing, "I love you, bayyybeeeee."

South of the Border

What's better than roses on your piano? Tulips in Skagit Valley! From Mount Baker to Bellingham and all the way down scenic Chuckanut Drive, there's plenty of sights to swoon over. And is it the proximity to Canada that makes everyone in these parts so dang nice? If bucolic is what you're after, a little jaunt up north ought to do the trick.

WAKE-N-LAKE

Want the delight of rounding bends to reveal wildflowers, the jaw-dropping beauty of mountain peaks, and to toss a snowball all at once? Load that backpack with water, trail mix, and fruit and set on out on a lovely adventure to **Mount Baker**. En route to the hike, make a pit stop at the **Glacier Public Service Center** for bathrooms, history on the area, and to purchase maps since cell service is spotty to nonexistent. Then, stop and check out **Picture Lake**, which earned every inch of her name with the stunning mountain reflection in the water. (Find out which trails are ADA accessible from the fantastically detailed "Accessible Adventures in the Pacific Northwest" YouTube

series from the Forest Service.) There are all manner of beautiful trails around **Heather Meadows**, but we suggest giving the **Bagley Lakes Loop**—a pretty chill two-ish mile circle with minimal elevation gain—a go. On the path, you'll encounter not one but two alpine lakes, swaths of flowers, and a year-round snowfield. And all of that with a looming mountain set behind you.

HOT TIP: Near-ish the mountain is the beloved North Fork Brewery, Pizzeria and Beer Shrine—an excellent spot to celebrate a successful hike via loaded pies and frosty IPAs.

TIPTOE THROUGH THE TULIPS

Let's talk tulips! The magical flowers that famously cast such a spell around the world for their beauty, tulips were even used as a form of currency in the late 1600s. Locally, they picked up steam big time at the turn of the twentieth century when George Gibbs, a farmer who'd immigrated from England, wrote our US Department of Agriculture and basically said, "Hey, dudes, help me grow some tulips. I think it could be really big." And the feds responded with, "Totes!" In 1905, the USDA imported fifteen thousand bulbs from Holland, and it was so successful that thus began a tulip test garden that ran for years, only closing due to the Great Depression and some bulb-killing winters. The test garden, however, led to a snowball of tulips in the area, and by 1955, the Washington Bulb Company became the leading bulb grower (that's tulip, irises, and daffodils) in all of North America.

That was the windup to talk about the annual **Skagit Valley Tulip Festival**, which runs the month of April, painting the area

with giant swaths of colors thanks to the pretty petals of garden tulips, parrot tulips, and striped tulips (said to symbolize a lover's beautiful eyes! Hawwwt.) There are multiple farms to run between (**Roozengaarde** has less kiddo activities and therefore less kiddos), so pick your vibe or do it all if you really love it.

After a morning galivanting through the flower fields, you'll be ready for some sustenance in the nearby town of La Conner, which hosts the majority of Tulip Fest–related events. In addition to its general postcard cuteness and museum options, there are tons of food choices near the historic waterfront area. If you can get there by three p.m., try **Calico Cupboard**, a cute little bakery with simple lunches. But the real point is to snag one of their enormous cinnamon rolls known as "the sweetest buns in town." That is, except for your honey's.

GO H.A.M.

From home fries smothered in salsa and sour cream to Greek tofu scrambles, consider starting the day with brunch at Bellingham's **Old Town Cafe**. Located on bustling Holly Street, the historic 130-plus-year-old building has been a restaurant in some shape or form for nearly one hundred of those years, and in the 1960s earned its rep as "a hippie spot."

As long as we're talking the '60s, you cannot leave the area without walking three hundred feet to visit **Aladdin's Antiques and Records** (aka **Aladdin's Lamp**) located below **Penny Lane Antique Mall**. You like affordably priced vinyl that goes on for miles? You gotta go. You like weird oversized lamps? You gotta go. Into old accordions? You get the picture.

Now let's swing the pendulum of activities and drive ten minutes to experience the beauty that is **Whatcom Falls Park**. This is a low-energy, high-rewards hike. Walk across the lovely Stone Bridge to see Whatcom Falls crashing into the water. From there, there are oodles of options depending on how long you want to walk—swim in the summer at **Whirlpool Falls**, watch ducks paddle about at **Derby Pond**, or check out the century-old train trestle.

When your stomach starts to grumble again, head back and hit the charming red-bricked historic Fairhaven neighborhood. More specifically, dinner at a place lauded over and over again, **Övn Wood Fired Pizza**. Their Neapolitan pizza—with yeasty dough and mozzarella that's hand stretched every day—gets a perfect char in their eight-hundred-degree wood-fired oven. And yes, there is carefully selected wine for a perfect mouth pairing.

BABY, YOU CAN DRIVE MY CAR

Nothing beats a scenic drive together. Good music, good conversation, and beautiful scenery. As far as scenic drives go, the twenty-mile **Chuckanut Drive**—Washington State's OG scenic byway—is one for the books.

Get onto the byway from Bellingham's Fairhaven neighborhood. BTW, if you need to fuel up before you go, hit **Magdalena's Bistro and Crêperie** for handcrafted crepes or *drool* traditional pan-fried Polish pierogis. Then head south, enjoying the view, until you soon come to **Larrabee State Park**. The first designated state park in Washington, Larrabee is a heckuva camping date if that's your vibe, but the strictly day visitors have all manner of activities here, too. Bring your bikes for fifteen miles of biking trails, dig for clams, spy the Amtrak trains rolling by, or sit on the beach and watch happy dogs frolic. All options are good options.

Continue south, stopping at pullouts for photos and take in the grandeur as you go. Keep an eye out for trumpeter swans as you slide into the unincorporated communities of **Bow and Edison** that seamlessly blend into each other. For a teeny place snuggled into the foothills of Blanchard Mountain, the ratio of great offerings is impressive. You can farm hop by hitting **Taylor's Shellfish Oyster Bar and Shellfish Market** for the freshest of seafood or go pick some plump treats at **Bow Hill Blueberries**. Wander into the little gallery and shops in the small intersection that is town. It's always wise to pay a visit to the loved and renowned bakery **Breadfarm** for hazelnut espresso shortbread or a Parisian baguette for carb-licious snacking. Itching for a little nightlife before you head out? **The Old Edison** has been in town since 1900 and is *the* spot for fun. The wood-paneled rec room from your childhood fills up with a band every weekend, and patrons can twirl in between shuffleboard games.

Islands of the North

Who doesn't love a hard-to-get-to archipelago? Ballers can holler for a seaplane, but the rest of us are just fine tootling up Whidbey Island, over Deception Pass, and waiting in Anacortes for a not always timely ferry. It ain't no thing. Set your restlessness aside and get on island time. You'll get there when you get there, and every second until then will be overflowing with jaw-dropping scenery. The San Juans are about as close as you can get to a dreamy Mediterranean holiday on this side of the planet. The climate's not quite the same, but lean back, breathe in that salty air, let your mind wander, and see where you might end up.

OK, before we dig into the island dates, we have to chat briefly about getting to the islands. Sit down, kids, this is your important FERRY TALK. The ferries are a magical thing. A car—which cannot float—drives onto a boat and then ends up on land again to keep vrooming. What?!

However, the system can be patience testing at best, patience busting at worse. Reservations? Umm yeah, you might be able to make some, but any mobile tickets they send you won't have dates and times on them, so have all that documented on your own. Need to get an earlier ferry than your reservation? Well, you can get into the standby line, but they'll inexplicably cancel your actual reservation and then if you don't make it, you now are out of luck altogether.

Furthermore, ferries that go west require paying, but eastbound ones don't. Interisland ferry travel is free for passengers, but not cars. And the myriad of other (sometimes difficult to find) details go on and on. Our best advice is to absolutely make advance reservations for any of the ferries that take reservations. Even if a ferry time is sold out, keep checking because people cancel and slots can open up even when it feels like you've lost hope. When it is your time, show up at least an hour early with a full water bottle and some snacks, and don't overplan your day because they often run late. If your date requires island hopping with a spendy boat tour around one island followed by strict dinner reservation on another with minutes to spare in between, forget it. You'll save yourself a lot of frustration keeping things loose, so once you are on your island of choice, choose to be chill and fun, which is an aphrodisiac in itself!

AYE-AYE, CAPTAIN

Feel the sigh of relief escape your lips as you enter into the relaxed rustic vibes of the **Captain Whidbey Inn**. Built at the turn of the last century, the madrona log lodge somehow feels both rickety and indestructible. It's a place full of these kind of juxtapositions—a super old stone fireplace anchoring a lobby where you can sip a delicious modern cocktail from the pretty horseshoe bar. Walls made from sturdy logs that are somehow also paper thin so you feel like you and your neighbors are in summer camp together (the shared bathrooms with clean, modern showers also strengthen the thought). Not into the *Little Darlings* vibe as much? That's OK, too. Opt for one of their chic standalone cabins with king-size beds, fireplaces, and a private porch to sit and drink your coffee while you blissfully stare out at Penn Cove.

There's a sweet garden with a little coffee shop for morning Joe and breakfast nibbles, lawn games aplenty around the grounds to induce some friendly competition, and free kayaks for a romantic sunset paddle. Settle on the deck of the **lodge restaurant** for a northwest-focused dinner menu to watch a sea lion swim by or a blue heron make a dramatic dive as they vie for the same unlucky fish. After dinner, wander into the lounge area, where the vibe is joyous and everything from M. Ward to Tina Turner plays on the speakers. Grab the two Etch A Sketches from the game shelf and attempt portraits of the other. Odds are they'll be awfully inaccurate but incredibly entertaining.

HOT TIP: Just west of Captain Whidbey's lobby, find the path with a little nook holding two Adirondacks and an intimate firepit overlooking the Sound for a private party of two.

As for daytime adventures in the area, make sure to go for a little stroll in the quaint **downtown of Coupeville**. Look familiar? If you are a person of exquisite taste, you will recognize it as the setting of the 1998 film *Practical Magic* starring Sandra Bullock, Nicole Kidman, Dianne Wiest, and Stockard Channing as a family of witches. (If that sentence doesn't fire your engines, something's going on.) The charming hundred-plus-year-old waterfront buildings were once livery stables and general stores, and now make for a delightful photo opp. Stop into **Toby's Tavern** for mussels from *right there* or **Little Red Hen Bakery** (which served as Sandy's biz in the movie) for house-made English muffin sandwiches and a sourdough chocolate chip cookie. Or traipse out onto the wharf to sip Italian sodas at **The Cove** coffee shop.

An adventure that cannot be missed is the trip up to **Deception Pass**. En route to the nearly four-thousand-acre state park (Washington's most visited!), take a quick detour in the town of Oak Harbor to grab a picnic lunch from the **Whidbey Island Bagel Factory**. The menu packs options, be it the classic lox and cream cheese combo on a rosemary chive sea salt boiled bagel to a Greek bagel loaded with artichokes and feta on a black olive and basil bagel. Yum!

Take your loot onward as you head over the marvelous and picturesque high bridge (look down if you're adventurous, and keep eyes pointed upward at all costs if you're scared of heights). Inside the park, there is no limit to activities. Forested trails with red rock quarries! An ADA accessible sand dune trail! Walk across the Deception Pass Bridge! It's not possible to do it all in a day (or a week), so many future visits are necessary, but a good place to start is the **Rosario Beach tide pools**.

There's a big grassy field to play bring-your-own badminton, and a lovely stone- and wood-covered picnic area to scarf dem bagels before you get to the water. The tide pools themselves are so popular with kiddos and anemone lovers that they have a roped-off path to keep visitors in line as they ogle urchins, sea stars, and crabs. Very VIP! Overlooking the tide pools is a giant wooden sculpture depicting the story of Ko-kwal-alwoot, **the Maiden of Deception Pass**. Read the plaques around the carving to learn the story from the Samish Indian Nation of how the young woman married a man from under the ocean and now brings abundance from the sea to her people. If you get hot and feel brave enough to jump off the dock into the chilly waters for a quickie plunge, first check for giant-ass jelly fish that just might be shimmying through the water! Or take your sun-loving selves over to **Cranberry Lake**, a freshwater lake right off North Beach that features slightly warmer waters and definitely less stinging creatures.

HOT TIP: Prepare to see Deception Pass in a new light by booking a nighttime bioluminescent kayaking trip where you'll paddle through the sparkling waters, thanks to tiny living organisms that produce and emit light. Fantastic!

ORCAS PORCUS

Let's talk about Orcas Island and its beauty. From the charming lavender fields to the adorable mandatory stop at **Orcas Island Pottery** to the fancy-pants mansions on the island (Oprah had one here) to the loaded shelves of **Darvill's Bookstore**, this is a cush weekend spot with lots of good options for fun and to lay your head.

For full splurge mode, try the luxe life at **Outlook Inn**, which has gotten all manner of shoutouts from the *New York Times* to *Kinfolk*. The Water's Edge suites are steps from Fishing Bay with beach access, wet bars, balconies, plush robes, and posh heated bathroom floors. There's a delightful little garden on the grounds and an equally cute cafe with a banging brunch menu.

Animal Lovers, take a look at the **Pebble Cove Farm Inn and Animal Sanctuary**, a place where you can both sleep on a little farm and be greeted each morning by ponies, pigs, and a turkey named Dread Captain Redbeard. Traditionalists, try out the **Kangaroo House Bed & Breakfast** (which once actually did house a pet kangaroo), the longest running B&B on the island, where the owners (Charles and Jill) whip up multicourse breakfasts for their guests each morning, like Alsatian potato pancakes stuffed with fresh veggies and herbs and gooseberry (from their garden) mousse topped with whipped cream and macadamia nuts while copious coffee and tea flow. They've been on the island for years and will happily indulge you in history or itineraries if you ask.

HOT TIP: Pedro the Lion! Fruit Bats! Shook Twins! See cool cats like these and more perform every year at the Doe Bay Fest, a music festival held on the thirty-eight acres of beautiful waterfront land at the Doe Bay Resort & Retreat.

Regardless of where you stay, there's some things that are must dos. During the day, that includes a scamper up to **Mount Constitution** (the tallest point in all the San Juans) and a hike around **Mountain Lake**. You can loop the whole thing for a bit of a harder seven-ish-mile loop with a climb, or you can just peep at the lovely lake and then head back at a leisurely pace. Don't want to hike at all? Drive up for a gorgeous sunrise view of Mount Baker with coffee in hand and sleep still in your eyes.

History buffs or folks who want a taste of George Clooney's Lake Como life should pay a visit to the **Rosario Resort & Spa**. The resort itself is spread over dozens of acres in different types of accommodations, but is centered around the original Moran Mansion, which is happily situated with manicured grounds atop a cliff with expensive ships sailing below. Built by former Seattleite mayor Robert Moran, who was in office during the great fire of June 6, 1889, there's a free small museum on the second floor open to the public that tells the tale of ritzy life on the island at the turn of the century.

In 1921, he donated twenty-seven hundred acres for the creation of Moran State Park. But he also knew how to party (oh, to be rich and funemployed). There was originally an indoor swimming pool filled with salt water, a maple bowling alley, a billiards room, and an oval organ room with a large stained-glass harbor scene. Before you head out, pop down to the **Rosario Marina** for a lunch of fresh seafood or a lovely watermelon and feta salad while sipping a local white wine and watching the rich people come in on their boats. You might even see a seaplane land. Funsies!!

The little town of Eastsound is in the middle of the island and makes for a splendid walk. While there, you should absolutely go to **Matia** for dinner. Named for a tiny island nearby that's a National Wildlife Refuge known for its mossy cedar trees and black licorice slugs, the cozy spot specializes in local cuisine—greens from the island! Gouda from around the corner! Cultured butter so rich you'll dream of it that night! And an omnivore's feast showcasing all the island bounty! Plus, cocktails to knock you on your butt in the best way.

IT'S FRIDAY (HARBOR) AND I'M IN LOVE

Friday Harbor on San Juan Island is charismatic from the second the ferry pulls up. Full of so many cute dogs it almost seems like a parade, and nary a fast-food chain in sight, the walkable port is a fun couple of hours for snacking, sunning, and getting an ice-cream cone. It's also the place to hop onto one of the many whale-watching tours in the area. Many of the tours work together to radio in whale spottings, so chances are good that you won't miss the boat if orcas are spotted.

One to try, packed full of nonstop nature info, is **San Juan Excursions**. It's a three-to-four-hour journey aboard the ***Odyssey***, a 1941 converted US Navy search and rescue vessel. In addition to the captain, there are multiple naturalists aboard who hand out binoculars and walk you through the history of the marine life on display. We're talking info on how a glacier carved the islands twelve to fifteen thousand years ago. We're talking which spot was Jacques Cousteau's second-favorite diving area in the world (if you are old enough to understand that sentence, don't forget to take your omega-3 pill). We're also talking about the difficult plight of the area's whales.

The fact is, whale-watching trips bring both sorrow and joy. The area's orcas are so starved due to overfishing of canneries and instillation of dams and myriad other reasons that the populations have dwindled to the point that the crew can name the ones you'll see, like Slick or Alki, based on their fins. Without action, it's conceivable there won't be orcas for future generations to see.

There is also hope in stories like that of Big Mama. No humpback whale had been seen in the area for nearly a hundred years thanks to the @#%& practices of nineteenth-century Euro-American whalers. Then one day, in 1997, Big Mama showed up to the surprise of all. Since then, she's returned from her annual Bone Zone time in Hawaii, often with a new calf by her side (seven and counting!) spurring the phrase "Humpback Comeback," which is *not* to be con-fused with "Humpty Dance." Now her babies are having babies, and everyone is thrilled to see the family grow. Mamas FTW.

HOT TIP: You can also opt for the joy of whale watching by not getting on a boat/contributing to the noise pollution the whales loathe by spotting our spouting friends from land. Lime Kiln Point is on the rocky bluff at the west end of island with a picture-perfect viewpoint.

More Fun

JAZZ HANDS!—Mondays can be a little quiet on the islands but not in darling Orcas Village, where horns fill the salty air every Monday night at Orcas Hotel's Jazz Supper Club.

DUCK DUCK SOUP—Covered in vines and tucked down a tranquil country road, **Duck Soup** serves up fancy farm-to-table fare from their swanky, miles-from-everywhere forest lounge.

PRETTY GIRLS MAKE GRAVES—The goths and LotR fans among us should take a short detour to the enchanting, if a little creepy, **John S. McMillin Memorial Mausoleum** on San Juan Island, also known as Afterglow Vista. Who knew a final resting place could be so pretty?

NOOD BEACH—Lopez Island is maybe the most chill of the easily accessible San Juans. For ultimate seclusion, head all the way to the southernmost tip and Point Colville, an almost tropical paradise known for its turquoise waters. It's a bit cold to dip, but if you do take the plunge, **Setsunai Noodle Bar** in Lopez Village will warm you right up.

WASTIN' AWAY—**Secret Cove** restaurant overlooking the Guemes Channel in Anacortes has nothing secret about it, but the upstairs bar does have a raucous happy hour dive feel known for its one-two punch of beer-battered fish and beer-battered locals.

Islands of the South

If you or yours are feeling cooped up in the city, it's not hard to board a ferry for a quick getaway. Sail off to Bainbridge, Vashon, or Bremerton and the rest of the Kitsap Peninsula and you'll feel the tension melting away. Or, if you're miraculously stress-free in this day and age, and just looking for an excuse to escape, there are plenty of festivities throughout the year to lure you away from your metropolitan nirvana.

GARDEN VARIETY

If you are certified Plant People, or at least, dabbling in the lifestyle, we declare the southern islands near Seattle an ideal place to appreciate flora of all kinds. Buying plants, admiring plants, learning about plants, it's all date worthy, so let's go!

Port Orchard

Brothers Greenhouses should be on your Port Orchard list. They have thousands of plants that range from a cute little houseplant you can buy together (start off easy with something like a spider plant and do not be swayed by the fickle fiddle-leaf fig on your first foray into #plantparent) to greenhouses stuffed with veggie starts, foxgloves, calla lilies, apple trees, and even a mini shelter dedicated to piles of dahlia tubers, fragrant onion bulbs, and seed potatoes.

On top of being an A-plus nursery, it sets itself apart through its many tiny fairy houses built into stumps with little creatures and succulents acting as trees and moss as grass. The pièce de résistance is the full **Hobbit House** built outside and complete with a round door, a working fireplace, a living roof, and an adorable spot to snap a possible holiday card photo.

Bremerton

When it comes to the art of bonsai, **Elandan Gardens** founder, Dan Robinson, is a rock star. If you're lucky enough to see him on-site of his waterside gardens—complete with ponds, waterfalls, and sculptures—tending to his babies, ask him about the stories of his favorites and you won't be disappointed. He'll tell you how he started training on bonsai in 1957 while working his way through college and has been mastering the craft ever since.

The three hundred bonsai trees around the garden live on their own special mantels, positioned up against the water of the Puget Sound, nature's version of a white-walled gallery. Most come with a placard outlining what makes them special. You'll see twelve-hundred-year-old trees carefully coiffed into a tiny work of art. Carved-out bougainvillea, contorted elm trees permanently waist high, and azalea bushes that have been trained into beautifully blooming little mini trees that Tinker Bell herself would want to live in. It's all a lovely walkabout if you just like pretty things, and if you're even mildly interested in trees, it's downright fascinating.

Bainbridge

One hundred fifty acres, fourteen different types of landscapes, one lush garden. Welcome to the **Bloedel Reserve**. (Cue *Jurassic Park* theme music.) It's not the type of botanical garden where each item is labeled and you learn its Latin name; rather, this is a peaceful meander through different lands created by a married couple, Virginia and Prentice Bloedel, who wanted to share the love with others. In fact, the reserve says Prentice was an early adopter of

the understanding of nature's therapeutic power, and funded psychological research on the emotional effect of spending time outdoors.

So it's entirely probably that he'd be thrilled for you to spend time in the **Moss Garden**, as verdant as can be, with forty different types of the springy stuff. Or the sculpted **Japanese Garden** designed by Fujitaro Kubota, of Kubota Garden fame (see page 53). Or perhaps the quiet beauty of the **Reflection Pool**, inspired by Finnish and English canal ponds. At the far end of the pool, a flat stone covering the buried ashes of Virginia and Prentice is inscribed with a line from an Emily Brontë poem: "Are not the best beloved of years around your heart forever?"

SHOW ME YOURS

What to do for a date night in Bremerton, you ask? Dinner at **Hound + Bottle**. Shaken cocktails adorned with an orchid garnish, buttery crusted potpies, and bucatini with briny Gaeta olives are all on the menu for this seasonally focused restaurant. Eat it all, maybe with some veggies for good measure. Then on to the theater!

Bremerton Community Theater has been entertaining locals and visitors alike since 1944 with its run of classic productions. You know, the ones you've heard of even if you're not a full-blown thespian. That means *Mary Poppins, Murder on the Orient Express,* and even the greatest comedy of all time, *Clue.*

FIESTA FOREVER

The folks around the Kitsap Peninsula like to party! At very specific times. Mark these festivals on your calendar now so you can remember the fun later.

May

Officially, **Viking Fest** celebrates the Scandinavian roots of downtown Poulsbo. But also we think a lot of the event's appeal stems from folks wanting to see how hot they look in a Viking helmet. Decide for yourself at the annual weekend fest that includes a parade with maidens on boat floats, Celtic music, and Norwegian dancers!

July

An all-volunteer-run event, Vashon's annual **Strawberry Festival** is a love letter to the GOAT berry, and to the island itself. There's a parade (including a cute kiddo parade), local vendors slinging goods, and even a bouncy house. On the main stage, enjoy three days of back-to-back bands running all day and into the night.

October

Knight, brute, reaper, and forest hag. These are just some of the characters you'll come into contact with at **My Haunted Forest**. Located in Vaughn at the **Grand Farm** and running each October, they bill this as a "medieval alternate reality with dragons and other mythical beasts lurking in the wood." Terrifying.

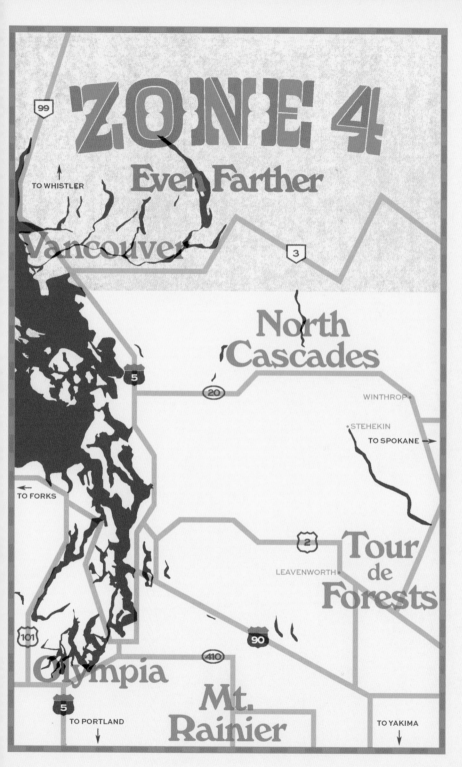

Vancouver

Once in a while, America does not bring the vibe. The next time the news gets you down, there's no better remedy than a last-minute trip to the Great White North for a quick dose of perspective. On a good day, you can get there quicker than you can watch *Harry and the Hendersons*. Stuff yourselves with delectable comfort foods and then walk it off at any number of world-class attractions. Don't forget to pack your passports and check the Canadian government's website for up-to-date entry requirements.

GRANVILLE ISLANDS IN THE STREAM

Once an industrial manufacturing area, Granville Island is now a spot for pleasant meandering through rehabbed old buildings full of bakers, boutiques, galleries, and seafood. The **Granville Island Public Market** is a fave for many of the same reasons as Pike Place Market. Along with bushels of fresh produce, there are aisles of vendors with fluffy coconut pies, Italian pastries, hot buns

(wink), and specialty foods among the hustle and bustle. Best to get an overall view before you pick your prize.

Eat your treat outside while watching some of the street performers pull off precarious acrobatics, jazz hands offer up a magic trick, and buskers play random instruments. Roam in and out of artists' studios, where you can see pottery wheels in action (hello there, favorite scene from *Ghost*), silversmithing, or hypnotic glassblowing at **Vancouver Studio Glass**. Take a load off at **Dockside Restaurant** (located at the Granville Island Hotel). The harbor view patio offers a boost of sunshine dotted with cabanas and sleep firepits, as well as primo viewing of boats coming and going against a spectacular backdrop of the city's skyline. Take advantage of daily early-afternoon happy hour for discounted highballs and fancy snacks.

Not ready to leave yet? Take in a show, darling! Granville Island is the hub of the city's theater community with multiple venues on-site. You can "yes, and" your way through a **Theatresports** competition with two improv teams pitted against each other to see who can make the audience, and judges, laugh more. Or go for a good old musical like *The Sound of Music* (the piece that taught us at an early age how sexy it is to hate fascism!) at the **Arts Club Theatre Company**.

HAPPY TRAILS

Is there anything quite as fun to eat as a dumpling? A squishy pocket of joy stuffed with your favorite fillings dipped in sauce that explodes in your mouth? Well, there's an entire date dedicated to the original Hot Pocket! A half an hour outside of Vancouver lies Richmond's **Dumpling Trail**, a collection of more than twenty restaurants offering steamed, pan-fried,

boiled, and deep-fried dumplings across cuisines. Chinese xiao long bao, Korean mandu, Vietnamese banh bot loc dumplings wrapped in tapioca skins, Japanese gyoza, and on and on. The best course of planning action is to hit the Visit Richmond tourism site, which offers multiple dumpling itineraries based on your mood, like Hidden Gems or Authentic Chinese Dining.

Now, to quote all Little League coaches when a kid gets whacked by a ball: "Walk it off, Champ." Carry your stuffed belly over to the **Richmond Night Market**, the largest night market in North America! It runs every Friday, Saturday, and Sunday from spring through fall, and is jam-packed with food and entertainment from more than five hundred vendors. On the food front (if you somehow have room left), vendors serve big ol' bowls of rainbow shaved ice and sushi tacos in nori "tortillas" and Vietnamese pizzas on grilled rice paper. This is all topped off with additional sensory stimulation like troupes of rainbow dancers, displays of big katana swords, and life-size animated dinosaurs.

STANLEY TUCCI MY BODY

Stanley Park is a cool date. The thousand-acre multi-recreational area was voted by Tripadvisor users as the top park *in the world,* which is a BFD, not

to be confused with BDE. Actually, maybe it's kind of both. If you're new to Vancouver's peninsula jewel, take the lackadaisical traipse around the park, which will totally be a nice time. Or you can front-load the fun a little bit by going in with a plan. If you're dating a perpetual Theater Kid (congrats!), stop by the **Shakespeare Garden** (snuggled up next to the also captivating **Rose Garden**) to see the park's interpretation of the Bard's work. The small arboretum contains trees name-dropped in his plays and poems, along with little plaques revealing the direct quote. Love trains? Hop on the little **Stanley Park Train**, a locally built replica of Canadian Pacific Railway Engine #374, squished down to barely-fitting-adults size. Why #374? In the late 1880s, that actual steam locomotive pulled the first transcontinental passenger train into town.

One stop for all is a sojourn to see the **First Nations art and the nine totem poles at Brockton Point**. The collection includes the **Rose Cole Yelton Memorial Pole** raised in 2009. A member of the Squamish Tribe, she was the last surviving member of the Brockton community living in Stanley Park until 1935. Her son, Robert Yelton, a Squamish carver, led a team of other carvers to create this symbolic piece. Interested in learning more about the totems? Consider booking a **Talking Totems Indigenous Art Tour** with the First Nations–owned **Talaysay Tours** to learn about the works with a cultural ambassador and trained Indigenous artist.

On the note of Indigenous art, opt for a stay at **Skwachàys Lodge Aboriginal Hotel & Gallery** located in Chinatown. Part boutique hotel, part art gallery, it goes the next step by offering on-site housing and studio space for twenty-four Indigenous artists. You can see the work in the street-level gallery and purchase a wide range of pieces—soapstone carvings, cedar weavings, and framed paintings, to name a few—

from dozens of First Nations artists. Each of the eighteen hotel rooms feature one-of-a-kind artist installations like a Tlingit hat theme or hummingbird motif.

The hotel is an easy walk to Gastown, where Victorian vibes and cobblestone streets make it a darling stroll through markets, shops, and galleries galore. One must-visit spot is **Pidgin**, an Asian French fusion restaurant where the plating feels worthy of defying the "food photos are so over" social media opinions. Talk to your server about which perfect Japanese Nikka whiskey (Black Label? Red Label?) to pair with your meal or maybe one of their signature sake flights? Heck, if you walked there, go for both.

GOLDEN HOUR

The specific part of this date is only available approximately three weeks out of the year, which means it's extra special. Imagine a hand-in-hand walk with your crush through a canopy of golden flowers dripping down on you, like a bunch of Roman gods and goddesses feeding you gilded grapes. This is the **Laburnum Walk** at the VanDusen Botanical Garden. In late May each year, its forty-three laburnum trees spring to life with hanging golden flowers from above and purple chives blooming up from below in a surreal image. Walk the dreamy walk, and tour the rest of the garden, including an Elizabethan hedge maze created from more than three thousand pyramidal cedars. Stop for lunch or an Aperol spritz in the open-air outdoor covered patio of the garden's **Shaughnessy Restaurant** before you go.

ADRENALINE CRUSH

Adventure lovers and adventurous lovers have long visited the area where the **Capilano Suspension Bridge Park** resides. In 1889, a Scottish civil engineer named George Grant Mackay decided to build a footbridge joining together the six thousand acres of forest he'd purchased on either side of Capilano River. A team of horses (who were most definitely not paid enough) swam a load of hemp rope across the river, where the ropes were then pulled up and anchored to huge cedar logs buried underground. That was the beginning of the hemp and cedar suspension bridge that folks came from all over to trounce across.

Nowadays the park holds a spot in the Canadian Tourism Hall of Fame. Literally, it was inducted in 2000. People still come from all over to walk the suspension bridge that sways 230 feet above the river. It's now fully rebuilt with modern safety equipment and has been featured in not one but two television masterpieces: *Psych* and *MacGyver*. That's range, baby! But there's more. You can also take a cool **Cliffwalk** on a cantilevered walkway somehow gripped to the side of the canyon for as Ewok an experience as you'll ever get. There's also the **Treetops Adventure**, which lets you run around 110 feet in the air on small suspension bridges through the rain forest.

Any time of year, this is going to be fun . . . or terrifying if you don't like heights. But imagine it lit up with half a million twinkling Christmas lights. Every year from mid-November to the end of January, **Canyon Lights** festivities take over. Walk the same cliffside paths at night with magic fairy lights wrapped around trees as high up as the eye can see. It's as romantic as can be, and attempting to walk mitten in mitten is A-plus adorable.

North Cascades

It's not easy to get to this national park for a large chunk of the year, and the rest of the time, it's teeming with adventure-seekers longing for an alpine rush that only this unreal corner of the world can supply. The good news is, it's not hard to lose the hordes. Nab a backcountry permit from any ranger station (or reserve online ahead of time) and make your way to the more than five hundred lakes and ponds or more than three hundred (for now!) glaciers this wonderland has on tap. For the less outdoorsy among us, there's no fee to take a leisurely drive, and cozy accommodations abound, but be advised, early birds catch the coziest worms—erm, rooms.

RANGE LIFE

The **North Cascades Scenic Byway** has more dramatic twists and turns than a telenovela. There might not be any characters pretending to be in a coma while also pregnant by their long-lost sister's husband, but there are jaw-dropping mountain views, picturesque lakes, and roaming horses that are equally entertaining. Too gnarly to cross in the winter, Highway 20 is only open in the summer, which is the perfect time to set out for a long weekend with plenty of time for frequent breaks to admire the scenery. Here are some of our favorite places to get out and stretch the legs and have some fun as you leave Seattle and head east. Mix and match them into your perfect trip.

Cascadian Home Farm Stand

You likely know the Cascadian Farm brand from grocery shopping; it all began at their twenty-eight-acre home farm. For five decades, byway cruisers have stopped here for fresh blueberry milkshakes and other decidedly summer treats.

Wildwood Chapel

Surrounded by big-leaf maple trees, the Wildwood Chapel is like a tiny home, but for churches. It can't even fit ten people and feels more dollhouse than church. It's also seen a lot of happy couples pass through its small doors, so maybe it's not a bad stop for practicing (or reminiscing about) the "You may now kiss" moment.

Ross Lake Resort

To enjoy the scenic view at Ross Lake Resort, you must channel the ethos of Donna Summer's "She Works Hard for the Money," because it ain't easy. First off, attempting to get a reservation at one of the rustic floating cabins—created from a leftover logging camp and after flooding the valley in 1952—with the twenty-two-mile lake stretched out in front of you takes patience. Every year, join the online waitlist with your date preferences and cross your fingers. Let's say you do get one of the coveted spots; to get to the resort requires parking on the highway at milepost 134, then walking a mile-ish down from the trailhead to a phone mounted to the last power pole. That's how you ring for the shuttle to come get you and jet you across the lake to your simple accommodations. But once there, with your rented canoe for lake paddling and a grand view of Pyramid Peak and Paul Bunyans Stump in the skyline, it'll feel worth it. Don't have the patience to wait for a room? You can do all the rigmarole for a day trip, too, including boat and canoe rentals.

Mazama General Store

For the last one hundred years, travelers have relied on the Mazama Store's various incarnations as a place to stock up for their vacation to the area. The family-owned store's current motto, "A little bit of everything good," does a solid job of detailing their offerings. It's a place to pull in for a sammie on fresh-baked bread and an Americano for the road. A spot to pick up some fresh greens from nearby farms and a jar of local butter for your cabin rental. Plus, shop the aisles for handmade crafts from the area—think pottery, woolen rugs, and jewelry. All in all, a heck of a pit stop.

Downtown Winthrop

We're a sucker for a town slogan, and Winthrop's "Adventure in the air with a certain western flair" really scratches that itch. It also means what it says, with an 1850s Old West aesthetic including antique boardwalks, false fronts, and saloons. There's beer to be drunk at the **Old Schoolhouse Brewery** and cinnamon rolls to be munched at the adorable **Sheri's Sweet Shoppe**. Mosey on over to the rare outdoor **Winthrop Rink** to practice your Pamchenko double moves, or more realistically, teeter precariously while sweetly holding hands and laughing. The best way to take advantage of the town is to stay overnight, and the reasonably priced cabins at **River's Edge Resort** come with private hot tubs overlooking the Chewuch River. This town is a great spot to stop after driving the scenic byway, though it's best known for its 120 miles of famed cross-country skiing trails. But to get here in the winter, you gotta go the southern route, because the byway is closed.

Sun Mountain Lodge

One of the old-school lodges of the PNW, built back in the 1960s, **Sun Mountain Lodge** has long been a spot for romantics, families, and friends to commune with nature and each other. We'll say up front, it's not cheap, but having a room here comes with a lot of possibilities. The resort is 3,000 acres of wilderness that includes a 120-acre private lake. It's also on the other side of the ridge, so it gets around three hundred days of sunshine a year, which sounds pretty nice during the Great Gray Times.

But what to do with all that space, you ask? In the summer, there is spectacular bird-watching with rufous hummingbird, belted kingfisher, and Barrow's goldeneye all flitting about. Hit the lake for all manner of water funtivities or go white-water rafting nearby on Methow River. The lodge also has a well-known horseback trail-riding program where you saddle up your steed and head out into nature with an experienced guide. Or rent a mountain bike and take off with a map to miles of trails that range from flat as a pancake to whoa nelly.

In the winter (again, you'll have to take the southern route), the lodge boasts the title of the first and largest destination cross-country ski resort in the country. You know what else is cute to try together? Snowshoeing. They have rentals and trail path maps ready to go for you. Then there's the best part of any winter trip, getting out of the snow for a hot toddy in the lodge by the fire.

Tour de Forests

"Diane, eleven thirty a.m., February 24th. Entering the town of Twin Peaks, five miles south of the Canadian border, twelve miles west of the state line. I've never seen so many trees in my life. As W. C. Fields would say, I'd rather be here than Philadelphia." Agent Dale Cooper had a thing for trees, and whether you're a transplant like he was or were born and bred in the Evergreen State (like Kyle MacLachlan was), chances are you're just as enamored by our majestic giants. Their forest magic draws us deeper into the state and even deeper into a state of awe. Grab a slice of cherry pie and a damn fine cup of coffee (or a bier and a brat if that's more your thing) and head off into the woods. May the forests be with you.

(LEAVEN)WORTH IT

You've likely heard of the charming Bavarian village of Leavenworth, even if you've never had the delight of walking a European main street smack in the middle of a Washington forest. The joy of this place, depending on the time of year you go, is that you can have wildly different experiences. In the winter,

it turns into a wonderland when backcountry skiers, ice climbers, and snowshoers hit the town for freezing activities galore. Unless you are OK with hordes of holiday crowds, we suggest going in January when the Christmas rush is over, but the town celebrates **Winter Karneval** all month long. That means half a million lights twinkling on buildings that all look like a place where Snow White might live.

If your winter wallet agrees, opt for the posh **Posthotel** overlooking the river. Their amenities setup is no joke, with a swim-out saltwater pool that sports little nooks and massaging jets, not to mention steam baths, saunas, and cold plunge pools to set your system right after a day of cavorting in the snow.

Bust out a different vibe in the summer by ditching snow activities for water ones. Book an affordable trip from **Blue Sky Outfitters** and meet the shuttle near downtown. From there, they'll bus you upstream of the Wenatchee River, hand you a blown-up inner tube and some Frisbees to use as paddles, and let you loose on the water. Be lazy and count the osprey flying overhead or jump in and swim next to your tube for a bit as the river gently guides you right back to the town's shore.

A more affordable accommodations option this time around is the **Hotel Pension Anna**, a small family-run hotel decorated with old-school Austrian and German furniture in each of the sixteen unique rooms. Stays include a complimentary German breakfast each morning that'll fill you up before you begin the fun times.

For a weekend summer stay, there are two required activities in the area. One is to make sure to grab a bratwurst (vegan sausages available!) and salty soft pretzel with mustard from **München Haus**. Then let a frosty beverage and the patio misters keep you cool. The second is to hit the town gazebo on a Saturday morning to see the **Leavenworth Alphorns** perform with their horns, which are traditional for Swiss herders and longer than a person is tall. It's a sight.

I WANNA HOLD YOUR CHELAN

The journey of getting to **Stehekin**—a little village nestled on the shores of Lake Chelan with no roads in or out—is part of the merriment. Hop on one of the "Lady" ferries from **Lake Chelan Boat Company** to take you further into the North Cascades, watching the big houses give way to more and more land. You can opt for one of their short layovers, but considering the length of time the ferry takes in and out, you'll feel more relaxed if you opt to stay for dinner and an overnight at **North Cascades Lodge**, conveniently located right at the landing.

WELCOME to STEHEKIN

LAKE CHELAN NATIONAL RECREATION ARE

Once you've disembarked, head to **Discovery Bikes** to get some wheels. Then set out on the little one-lane road that meanders around the lake and is bordered by hundred-foot trees towering overhead. You'll pass a little garden that you can pop out to visit, but the real destination is the **Stehekin Pastry Company**. Here, nearly everyone in the seventy-five-person town, plus all the ferry folk, seem to come together at lunchtime to chow sandwiches on fresh bread, sourdough pizza, and lots of deli salads. Sit out on an Adirondack and munch until you feel ready to keep on riding, then set off for **Rainbow Falls**. This gorgeous waterfall emits such a spray that when combined with the sun, it shows off by making rainbows for all to see.

AUDREY HORNE-Y

Twin Peaks fans typically fall into two camps. Those who watched it at some point in the '90s and remember it as being a good show with an explosive impact on pop culture. Or those that can't order a cup of coffee without calling it "damn fine" and regularly wiggle dance to the sultry sounds of Julee Cruise in their living rooms. Regardless of which camp you fall in, start the buildup for this adventure by rewatching the show from the start. The fashion alone is worth it. Agent Dale Cooper's fly trench coat, Bob's iconic denim on denim, and Audrey Horne's sweater game are all inspirations.

Once you're reacquainted with the original thirty episodes of Lynchian drama, get on out there for a *Twin Peaks* date extravaganza! There is, of course, the iconic waterfall from the show's opening credits, the 270-foot **Snoqualmie Falls**. An incredibly popular tourist attraction, there is a small park, observation deck, and, atop the falls, **Salish Lodge & Spa**.

You'll recognize the exterior as "The Great Northern Hotel," where Agent Cooper set up camp in room 315. The interior won't match up to what you're expecting (those scenes were shot at the **Kiana Lodge** in Poulsbo), but that doesn't stop Salish Lodge from offering a Great Northern Escape package, which includes a one-night stay, two Dale Cooper cocktails upon your arrival, and even a keepsake log pillow they bill as "compliments of the Log Lady."

Another can't-be-missed locale is "The Double R Diner," a.k.a. **Twede's Cafe**, a short drive away in North Bend. 'Twas at these hallowed Formica tabletop booths that cherry pie and coffee became forever associated with Washington. Thirty years later, you can still get the dessert combo that's as delicious as Coop said.

That covers the biggies, but say you want to go *deep*. In that case, we recommend booking a trip with **Twin Peaks Tour**. Owner David Israel has meticulously mapped out locations from all seasons of the show (and the movie), and you can choose which locations to focus on. You'll hit the ones above, but also see "Packard Sawmill," "Twin Peaks High," and so much more, along with a wealth of info about each iconic location. A superb gift and date for a superfan.

JOUST THE TWO OF US

At **Camlann Medieval Village** in Carnation, the year is always 1376. Archers pull back bows to let arrows zing. Potters use their feet to spin the wheel while crafting ceramics. Fuzzy sheep "baa" from behind a log fence. And *committed* actors juggle flaming torches, wear authentic costumes, and speak in ye olde English.

Officially, it is a living history museum dedicated to helping visitors (and kids on field trips) to understand what fourteenth-century rural England life was like. Unofficially, it's a *vibe*. On its monthly festival days, it draws a bus-

tling crowd keen on seeing all the above demonstrations plus black-smithing and knight competitions! Spend a couple of hours jaunting through the small village before you land in the **Bors Hede Inne** for an authentic meal made from era-appropriate recipes like "fenberry pye" or vegetarian "blamanger" rice dish. Verily, there is mead, and throughout the meal, expect minstrel songs and stories, accompanied by the lute.

More Fun

FAKED ALASKA—
Catapulted into the national
spotlight at the dawn of the '90s
when it stood in for backwoods
Alaska on TV's *Northern Exposure*,
the mountain town of Roslyn is like an
aged prom queen who likes to remind you
of her title. Which is to say, she's a whole lot of
fun. Stop into the Brick Saloon, one of the state's oldest,
as evidenced by the twenty-three-foot spittoon that still
sits at the foot of the bar. And for a weirdly good time,
keep an eye on the calendar for its annual spittoon boat
race in the spring.

#2 BEST HIKE—For pristine summit views with rel-
atively little effort, hike the hilariously named **Poo Poo
Point**, where you might catch paragliders launching off
into the wild blue yonder. For the record, the region is
named after the sound the steam whistle made back in the
days of logging.

A FOURTH TO BE RECKONED WITH—Even if
we have a long list of issues on how we want America to
do better, sometimes a good ol' fashioned Fourth of July
parade can still tickle your patriotic fancy. For a slice of
small-town Americana, post up for the day at the **Great
Carnation 4th of July Celebration**. The kiddie parade
might even make you hopeful.

GOOD THINGS COME IN TREES—A popular wed-
ding destination just south of Fall City, **TreeHouse Point**
opens up stays on weekends when there is not a private
party booked, but since there are only seven tree houses,
each more whimsical than the next, nabbing one takes
some patience. If you can get away during the week, you
might have better luck.

Mount Rainier

Not many can brag about having a bona fide volcano in their backyard. On sunny days, she is a beauty to gaze upon, her magnificence beckoning us to get up close and personal. But like all of nature, she can be dangerous if not taken seriously. Plan your trips accordingly and keep an eye on your weather apps, as the atmospheric conditions here have a mind of their own. For a more intimate experience, visit at the very beginning or end of the high summer season when smaller crowds make space for a diverse range of wildlife and the mountain's moodier side comes into full view.

TWO TICKETS TO PARADISE

Not only is a trip to Mount Rainier—a stratovolcano who does as she pleases with endless trails, views, and wildlife—a great time, the route to getting there is fun in and of itself.

At the **Northwest Trek Wildlife Park** near Eatonville, find a 723-acre wildlife park home to grizzly bears, a watermelon chompin' porcupine, a sweet red fox named Jack, herds of Roosevelt elk, stunning bison, and Carly the cougar. Unlike a zoo, the park features a 435-acre free-roam area where the animals (that get along) hang out. You can cruise through part of it on a self-drive tour in your car or book a Jeep tour with one of the naturalists to hear more detailed information about all the cool creatures in the park. Two pro tips: One, go in the spring for baby animals season (!). And two, follow the park's TikTok for daily serotonin boosts.

Also in Eatonville and worth a pop in is the uber-quaint **Mill Haus Cider Co.** Named for the old lumber mill in the town, the taproom's log cabin vibes,

the lovely lawn with ample outdoor seating, and the picturesque water mill make this a heckuva cute place for a leg stretch. If you're into crisp ciders made from locally grown apples, you can happily find everything from a habanero lime to the crowd-favorite huckleberry. Hearty flatbreads and salads are on the menu, making it a good lunch stop regardless of your cider preferences.

Get on **The Road to Paradise**, which is not our attempt at innuendo but the actual can't-miss circuitous route up the south slope that's rife with heart-stopping views. Once you hit the aptly named Paradise area, pay a visit to the **Paradise Inn**, a handsome old lodge with massive exposed cedar logs and a towering grandfather clock. Then hop onto the **Nisqually Vista Trail** for what some folks swear hosts the best explosion of wildflowers anywhere in the world. Eye candy abounds: colorful splashes of magenta Indian paintbrush, sunny yellow monkey flowers, and happy purple lupine-saturated meadows with thousands of flowers (plus larkspur, shooting stars, lilies, and so many more) as if a rainbow exploded onto this plot of earth.

To maximize your time in the area, you may want to consider hunkering down for a night or two. Three miles away from Rainier's southwest entrance lies **Wellspring Spa and Woodland Retreat**. The sprawling grounds resemble an adorable elfin village with overgrown gardens, a stone labyrinth, communal firepits, and a cluster of cabins ranging from ramshackle to bam(!)shackle. Opt for one of the newer builds, with soaring log ceilings, a

PARADISE

reading loft with a napping hammock, and gorgeous river-rock fireplace, and forgo the additional hot-tub fee because your cabin comes with a jetted heart-shaped soaking tub right in the main room. Go for long walks in the forest, read aloud to each other, and get super relaxed. This Wi-Fi-free, cell-service-free spot is for enjoying nature (and each other).

Though the cabins come with kitchens, it's worth a venture out to try the local cuisine or take a break from cooking. At **Copper Creek Inn**, devour sandwiches on thick sliced homemade bread and lust-worthy pies inside this storied local haunt. The wall mural of deer grazing before an alpine lake at the base of a snowy Rainier was painted by a neighbor but could definitely be on display in a hip art show. And don't leave the area without a visit to the seasonally open **Wildberry Restaurant**. Owned by Lhakpa Gelu Sherpa, who not only holds the world speed record for Mount Everest by hitting the summit in just under eleven hours, he's climbed the dang thing *fifteen* times! For half the year, his wife, Fulamu, serves up both typical American grub and Himalayan specialties, then they close to tend to their other restaurant in Kharikhola, Nepal.

If you're not the type of couple to trek the famous ninety-three-mile Wonderland Trail, which requires nearly two weeks (screaming emoji face) and a hard-to-get permit, try coming to the chill life with a ramble through the **Grove of the Patriarchs**. It's an easy breezy 1.5-mile round-trip hike through a Tolkien-level of wilderness magic. Take a fun suspension bridge over the Ohanapecosh River to an island of grand Douglas firs, western red cedars, and hemlocks. Their little island location has protected them from fires over the years, allowing them to thrive, with some more than one thousand years old and one nearly fifty feet in diameter. Trees are the bee's knees!

HOT TIP: Since the 1970s, Packwood's four-day annual Labor Day Flea Market is a scene and then some. Thousands of visitors flock to the small town to comb through tent after tent of crafts, antiques, dishware, old birdhouses, and other oddities.

Olympia

Rebel Girls (and those who love them), be advised, while the house parties and pop-up punk shows of yore are a little different these days, the same quirks that made Olympia ground zero for a revolution all those years ago are still alive and kicking. If your speed is a little less Kill Rock Stars and a little more K Records, consider a Sunday drive along the Thurston Bountiful Byway. Spoiler alert: this leisurely ramble is doable any day of the week!

"IT'S THE WATER"

The lovely little nature walk around **Brewery Park at Tumwater Falls** feels almost too good to be true. For the price of *free*, couples can galivant around a lovely path dotted with bright rhododendrons and full canopied trees while the gushing falls at the beginning of the hike cascade down into a burbling river companion as you continue. Bring your partner a nice coffee or tea for the walk and you've got a solid five-dollar date (very handy if you go on a lot of first dates).

The trail itself is only a half mile long, but the dual pathways on both sides of the river provide a disproportionate amount of entertainment to the length. Another way to say that is size doesn't matter here. With land most recently occupied by the now closed Olympia Brewing Company, whose headquarters and brewing area were perched above the east bank of the river, it's still privately owned by the nonprofit Olympia Tumwater Foundation. The green space features charming footbridges, a spot where lovers have left their padlocks Parisian-style, salmon fish ladders, little mini waterfalls on the sides of the path trickling through the trees, and oh so many historic plaques (the sexiest part of any date!). But, it is truly interesting to learn how a German immigrant from Montana, Leopold Schmidt, used the artesian wells of Tumwater to create some of the twentieth century's most popular beer.

BYWAY TO HEAVEN

The Thurston Bountiful Byway is a sixty-mile loop dotted with family farms and their stands, craft breweries and wineries, and a wide range of nature festivities. At the front of the line for your date? **Mima Mounds**!

Now, as per usszzzhhh, this is typically where we give you some sassy background on how this lil' gem came to be. But, in this case, we cannot. That's because no one really knows for sure what created these large mounds, which are often beautifully covered in wildflowers, that you can see up close on an easy half-mile path. Since the 1800s, this domed dirt has been a free-for-all of speculation, with ideas ranging from aliens to earthquakes, but now some geomorphologists declare it must be the work of generations of pesky gophers pushing upward. Cue the *Caddyshack* memes!

Keep on truckin' to the funkiest quarry around, the **Tenino Quarry Pool**. In the nineteenth century, this was a working sandstone quarry in the area where fellas hauled rocks out of the earth. The story that's been passed down is they struck a spring one day that filled the pit with water so quickly they had to haul butts out of there, leaving equipment behind that still sits ninety feet below the surface. Nowadays it's a fun stop on the byway to hop in for a cheap swim (there's a low admission fee) in the freshwater quarry with a little stream of water trickling down the rock side. It's an expansive pool at nine hundred feet by sixty feet, so even with a throng of folks, you can find room to doggie paddle.

Our final recommendation requires an advanced reservation, as the furry guests are particular about their visitors. We're talking about **Wolf Haven**, a rescue and accredited sanctuary that not only provides homes for displaced, captive-born wolves who cannot survive in the wild but also works to protect the remaining wild wolf population and their habitats.

The sanctuary also pushes forth a goal of educating the tens of thousands of visitors who roll through on the value of wildlife, and specifically the three species of North American wolves. Because of obvious reasons, most of us have never had the opportunity to see a wolf up close, but on these guided tours, you get to know each wolf and their backstory of how they came to live at the sanctuary. When one moves in, they stay the rest of their life with a team of staff and volunteers on-site dedicated to making the rest of their days good. Getting to see the statuesque creatures up close is a special treat unto itself, but occasionally one will give a spine-tingling howl. *Aaaaoooooooooooohhh.*

HOT TIP: Speaking of animal conservation, every Earth Day, Olympians hold the Procession of the Species, an utterly fantastic parade of animal-themed costumes, puppets, and floats. You might see a kooky crab float, a group of dancing bumblebees, or three kids carrying a makeshift cardboard snake. It's cool.

GET IT, GRRRL

Those of us lucky enough to have grown up in the PNW in the early 1990s were blessed to watch the rise of Nirvana in real time, learn about riot grrrl music from our friend's cool older sisters, and hoard neck chokers. Anyone outside the upper-left corner of the country might not know what a big role Olympia's **Evergreen State College** played in making formative feminist punk rock with members of Bikini Kill, Le Tigre, and Sleater-Kinney all on campus around that time. You can take a walk through the campus should you need inspiration for your own band—it's open to the public and there's even a self-guided tour available on the school's website.

Then it's time for **Rainy Day Records**, a place where time stands still. Selling records to clever shoppers since 1973, they have turntables, cassette tapes, and even one of those poster Rolodex thingies you flipped through as a kid. Plus, there are bins upon bins of vinyl to comb through (with plenty of riot grrrl music on hand), and a good ol' listening station to cue it up before you take it home. As long as we're talking important forms of creative outlet, we cannot understate the importance of zines to the era. They are snapshots of a cultural moment in the form of pasted-together articles and collages photocopied and shared among friends. The **Olympia Timberland Library** has a rad collection of more than seventeen hundred zines available for you to check out. They have old *Hot Pants* zines from the '90s, a trove of early '00s items, and keep adding to the collection with newer finds like *Paw Lick'r* and *Birth Control: Some Advantages*.

ZONE 5

A Real Commitment

Sea to Sky

Royal Isle

Olympic Loop

Eastern Washington

Portland

Sea to Sky

For some scenic highway branding to rival our own Mountain to Sound, look no further than British Columbia's Sea to Sky Highway. No matter the time of year, the views do not disappoint. And while Whistler is known the world over as a winter wonderland, you'd be remiss not to experience what the other seasons have to offer. Whether you're the type of couple (or throuple, no judgment!) who goes hard or the type that hardly goes at all, the road is sure to lead to your own little slice of heaven.

HIT THE ROAD, JACQUES

From the blissful moment you make it through the border lines, it's only about a two-ish-hour drive up to Whistler. And boy, is it a pretty one. The Sea to Sky Highway is some of the finest road-tripping around with forest cliffs on one side and water stretching out on the other. Make the most of the drive by popping out for little stops along the way, with the first a visit to **Sewell's Marina** on the **Howe Sound**. Here you can assuage your need for speed by renting a speedboat with only a driver's license and jet on out to explore the area. Cruise over to **Pam Rocks** to see a colony of rotund sea lions basking and admire the **Point Atkinson Lighthouse**. Don't feel comfy driving a boat yourself? They also offer a highly rated guided tour that only requires that you hop on and relax.

From one cool way of ogling water to the next, move north to the lovely **Shannon Falls Provincial Park**. At more than a thousand feet tall, this waterfall offers a majestic view, and the fact that it's mere steps from the parking lot with nearby public restrooms make it nearly impossible to skip. On a hot day, cool off with a stroll through towering sun-blocking trees while the falls' fairy mist floats all around.

HOT TIP: For an affordable overnight option, the Klahanie Campground is right across the road from Shannon Falls. Some spots can even see it out their tent windows, while others are waterfront to Howe Sound, and some are a little ho-hum. Consult the map carefully before booking!

Next up? Sharing the eagle-eyed views at the **Sea to Sky Gondola**. Hop into one of the neon and glass cubes from base camp before going up, up, and away. Spot the little dots that are windsurfers at the end of the Sound or stare at the snowy mountain peaks at eye level until it feels like you are high enough to high five whoever's in charge at the pearly gates. Once you hit the summit, get a further adrenaline rush by walking across the bouncy, death-defying three-hundred-plus-foot-long **Sky Pilot Suspension Bridge**, which offers you views of the entire world in all directions.

HOT AND HEAVY

A day date at **Scandinave Spa Whistler** is like taking a ton of horse tranquilizers without any of the side effects (don't ask how we know). From the second you arrive at this indoor/outdoor twenty-five-thousand-square-foot Nordic spa nestled in the forest, your heart rate slows and your body involuntarily starts to chillax. After checking in for your robe and slippies, you learn the best rule you didn't know you needed: no talking and no cell phones. That means within minutes you can fully give yourself over to the quiet of the trees as you begin a hydrotherapy cycle that's spread across three acres with little buildings and pathways all around.

Lead off by getting hot. That could be in one of the outdoor hot tubs, or through breathing in the heavenly eucalyptus smell in a fully fogged steam room, or by stretching out in the giant sauna with a roaring fire inside. The heat melts away knots in the muscles, increases blood flow, and sweats out the stress. Second step is to cold plunge, said to flush toxins, tighten the pores, and release endorphins. Options for this include an icy Nordic waterfall, cold shower, or a quickie plunge in a freezing tub. Each require a bit of bravery for a few seconds, but trust the process. The end step is perhaps the easiest: zone out. Technically you're letting your cardiovascular system regulate itself, but you'll also want to simply . . . be. This might be where Scandinave's star shines brightest. There are solariums with easy chairs facing the sun. There are crackling indoor and outdoor fireplaces to rest in front of. There are hammocks swinging in the trees, which might induce a full public nap. The best part of this whole experience is that once you're done tree napping, you go right back and do the whole cycle again and again.

I WILL FOLLOW YOU INTO THE DARK

Vallea Lumina is a little bit forest nymph, a little bit mystery, and a little bit like the one really cool part in the Peter Pan ride at Disneyland where you're flying through the stars. Couples show up at nightfall to this woodland light installation excursion to "follow cryptic radio transmissions and the lingering traces of two long-ago hikers to find the scenic trailhead where the real journey begins." Oooh!

Once you've been sworn in as a deputy ranger, your job is to look for the long-gone missing hikers and any clues that might help solve their disappearance as you go further into the trees *X-Files* style. Along the way, you discover forest guardians, magical campfires, and stars that dip down from the sky as two realities blend into one. It's a lovely otherworldly kind of evening made even better if you can turn off the logical part of your brain and give into the wizardry of it all.

A REASON FOR ALL SEASONS

No doubt when you first heard of Whistler's draw, it involved skiing. Which, like, fair. **Whistler's Blackcomb ski resort** is the largest in North America, with a couple of million visitors a year practicing their pizza and french fry

moves. More than that, Whistler hosted all the alpine skiing events during the 2010 Winter Olympics, so it is the legitest of legit.

Regardless, whether you are a super skier or fall down just by looking at a snowflake, you can take advantage of all the alpine village has to offer, namely sports bars, dance floors, fancy dinner hot spots, and a *lot* of outerwear shopping opportunities. Plus fabulous hikes, lakes to jump into in the summer, and killer bike trails. There's also the world-record-breaking **Peak 2 Peak Gondola** that can take you between Whistler Mountain's **Roundhouse Lodge** and Blackcomb Mountain's **Rendezvous** (two spots offering food with unparalleled views). In eleven minutes, you'll go from one mountain to the next, suspended fifteen hundred feet above ground. It's a multi-Guinness record holder as the world's longest unsupported span for a lift of this kind, the world's highest lift of its kind, and the world's longest continuous lift system. It's also super scary and super cool.

Not sure when to go? Take a look at Whistler's highly scheduled party calendar, as there always seems to be some kind of shenanigans about to take place. Every January, the town hosts the **Whistler Pride and Ski Festival**, a week of queer celebration that includes a parade, tons of skiing, and parties galore. July begins with a bang on Canada Day with a parade and outdoor symphony concerts and fireworks, which then kicks off the **Whistler Summer Concert Series**. Tourists and locals can take advantage of the free outdoor concerts in Whistler Olympic Plaza all summer long.

Once fall comes calling, it's beer o'clock with the **Whistler Village Beer Festival**. In one weekend, three thousand people descend upon the town to guzzle concoctions from dozens and dozens of breweries. And, of course, in the spring, there is the **World Ski & Snowboard Festival**. Every April, the area goes hard with the event, the largest annual winter sports and music festival in North America. Some folks call it the snowpeople's version of Burning Man, which really tells you all you need to know. Have fun, kids.

Eastern Washington

Whether you've been together for a few weeks or a few years, get to know your partner better with a long drive to the undulating hills and lonesome high-desert setting of Eastern Washington. Here, award-winning wines come with vistas to match, and the curious will be rewarded with oodles of fresh delectables. Cover yourself in mud, hop on a horse (or have a goat hop on you), and load up on wild shrooms. Have you lost your mind? No, you've just found your way to bountiful Eastern Wash.

BETTER YOURSELF

Therapy is a good thing. Solo therapy, couples therapy, and in this case, mud therapy. Smack in the middle of the state, **Soap Lake** is a destination for eastern European tourists because of its famed health benefits. It has some of the highest mineral content of any lake in the world, making the water oily and the mud nutrient rich; the shore can foam like you put a gallon of detergent into the washing machine. People have long flocked to this area to soak in the waters, paint themselves with mud, and lie out in the sun to let it draw out arthritic pain, skin issues, liver cirrhosis, you name it. Before readily available antibiotics, this *was* the doctor's office. Go for a soak and cure what ails ya.

In a surprising twist to some for a small rural town, Soap Lake also boasts the longest-running community theater in the county, going strong since 1979. The story of **Masquers Theater** reads like a movie script: a Californian family moved to town, bringing their love and experience in community theater along with them, started a troupe, and then left. But the town had been bitten by the bug and pulled together to keep it alive, moving from building to building while continuing to stage performances the artistic director hoped would inspire and provoke the rural community. It worked, with the theater raising the necessary $200,000 in community donations to build a permanent home. See for yourself how theater grabs ahold with one of their performances of classic stories such as *The Curious Savage, Noises Off,* or *The Picture of Dorian Gray.*

REGULATORS MOUNT UP

If you like vino, no doubt you've been on a wine tasting tour before. But have you ever done it by horseback? The peeps at **Red Mountain Trails Winery** had the idea to take visitors looking to tour the Red Mountain AVA—that stands for American Viticultural Area and basically means "wine time!"—on a horseback farm crawl. Take a one-hour horsey tour through the area known for lovely Cabernet Sauvignons, Syrahs, and Merlots (try not to quote *Sideways* around the Merlot). A newer wine area that began in the 1970s, Red Mountain has grown quickly and now is home to multiple vineyards with rows of grapes stretching out for what seems like miles. Each has its own personality, for example, the stunning grounds at **Hedges Family Estate**, which looks plucked from the French countryside.

Once you're back at Red Mountain Trails, there's more fun to be had. If it happens to be baby goat season, check to see if they're offering the absolutely adorable **Baby Goat Yoga** experience, where you can stretch out the bod while a little kid jumps up on you. The session ends with a farmer foot soak with Uncorked Cowgirl goat milk bath bombs and more baby billy goat cuddles. They are also a winery in addition to being an animal hang spot, so end the day on the ranch's expansive outdoor pavilion sipping a bold Bordeaux varietal next to a campfire, stuffy wine attitudes nowhere to be found.

FARMER FUN

Some impressive fast facts about the Yakima Valley:

1. With ninety organic farms, it has the most in the state
2. With forty commercial crops and a thousand different varieties of fruits and vegetables, it has the biggest assortment of fresh produce in the entire Pacific Northwest
3. It's home to the glorious **Los Hernández Tamales** and their world-famous (and seasonal) Yakima-grown asparagus and pepper jack cheese tamales.

Now that you've got the most important facts down, let's talk about a day of farm hopping. With three thousand total farms in the area, there's no way to do them all in a day/week/month, but you can choose a region and tackle a few at a time. In the Lower Yakima Valley, check out the **Yakama Nation Fruit & Produce** stand to pick up sweet-smelling nectarines and famed pickled asparagus from their Broken Spear label. **Prosser Farmers Market** has rows of ripe melons and freshly cut flowers alongside locally made granola and cheeses.

But then there's the Upper Yakima Valley, which has the **Downtown Yakima Farmers Market**, where as many as three thousand folks might show up for jarred honey, strawberries dripping with juice, and wild morel mushrooms. Head to **West Valley U-Pick** to pick your own apples in the fall and then press them into cider with an old-fashioned hand crank. In this fertile Eden, the options are limitless, and knowing where to start can be overwhelming. Take a peek at the tourism board's handy planning tool at visitfarmfreshfun .com to put an itinerary together and see what festivals (like Pumpkin Palooza!) are coming up.

PLAN B

Going to a show at the **Gorge Amphitheater** is likely already a part of your core memory; it has hosted a banging history of shows—Lollapalooza! Lilith Fair! Sasquatch!—since expanding to a twenty-thousand-capacity amphitheater in the early '90s. If for some reason you've never been, it's a vastly different experience than Climate Pledge Arena, with sweeping views of the Columbia stretching out in front of you and stars twinkling as you rock out into the night.

One way to amp up a visit to the area is to spend some time at the gorgeous (see what we did there?) **Cave B Estate Winery** right next door. Sip a glass of their red blend on the patio overlooking one of the most breathtaking views a drinking spot could ever offer. On concert days, they don't take reservations, but you can try your luck dropping in for a slice at the pizza truck out front and or a glass of wine from the folks pouring in the back. It's also a cushy place to crash after a concert. Once all connected, the business is now split between the Cave B winery and the separate spa and lodging. **Sagecliffe Resort & Spa** offers yurts with king-size beds and bathrooms, and cliff houses overlooking the river for when you wanna rage hard at a show but also need your beauty sleep.

Portland

Atop Portland's iconic Union Station, a blazing neon sign declares, "GO BY TRAIN." And if you've spent any time traveling down the I-5 corridor in the last few decades, you'll know that even a capricious railway system beats having to sit in that nasty Tacoma/JBLM traffic. For a complete roundup of how to spend a few hours (or a few years) in the Rose City, might we suggest seeking out a copy of *The Portland Book of Dates*? For a specially curated weekend within close proximity to the train station, read on.

PDA IN PDX

Want to take a little weekend trip down to Portland and not have to think about what to do? Let us lay out the easiest two-day feeding and frolicking frenzy. You already know the tiny dimension of highway hell on a Friday afternoon, so we say skip it. Instead, opt for the train. More specifically, book passage on **Amtrak's Coast Starlight train**, where swivel seats face the window and instead of teeth-grinding traffic, you can hang out, get a card game going, or play footsie!

A ten-minute walk or a blink-and-you-missed-it cab ride later will put you at **The Hoxton** hotel (nearby **Society Hotel** is a more affordable option with a cute on-site cafe). Line up a dinner reservation for its rooftop restaurant, **Tope**, where you can knock back killer tacos and margs in the lovely tiled space or—if warm weather is in play—on a patio with sweeping views of the city. You're well within your rights to call it a night right there. But if you do desire more, hit a show at one of the many venues within a coin's toss from the hotel: **Darcelle XV** drag cabaret to pay homage to the world's oldest drag queen, **Star Theater** for cumbia or psychedelic rock shows, or the famous floating floor of the **Crystal Ballroom** for big-name bands.

The next morning, get a coffee and a pastry in the lobby to tide you over until **Maurice** opens at eleven a.m., when you can tuck into a long, leisurely lunch. Here the swoopy handwritten menu offers French and Norwegian fare like radishes with salted French butter, oysters on the half shell, or cottage-cheese-and-tomato-topped smørbrød. Oh, and more pastries! Sit at the tiny  counter and watch the stripe-shirted servers whiz about like frenzied contestants on an episode of *The Great British Bake Off*.

Now you're off to begin a day of either window-shopping or actual shopping (reminder, Oregon has no sales tax, baybeee!). Within a few blocks, indulge in some of Portland's most beloved local brands. There's **Wildfang**, the feminist brand's flagship store, where you can pick up one of their iconic jumpsuits and carve your names like lovestruck teenagers into the wooden graffiti wall. **Danner** is there for when you need new hiking boots. When Portlanders need something slick, for years, they've relied upon both **Frances May** and **Machus**—two local boutiques that carry the hippest of designers as well as their own stylish in-house lines. Feeling spicy? **Spartacus Leathers** is the city's family-owned sex shop with toys, furry handcuffs, and the absolute best selection of come-hither fishnets around (plus a lotta great fashion for pride parades).

HOT TIP: Get to town a little early on Friday or not in the mood to shop on Saturday? A five-minute walk from The Hoxton is the utterly stunning Lan Su Chinese Garden—a botanical garden featuring rare plants native to China, beautiful stonework, and a fantastic Teahouse in the Tower of Cosmic Reflections.

Let's say you saved a little money from that lack of sales tax. Great. You're gonna need it now. To get into the members-only **Multnomah Whiskey**

Library, you can buy a one-night hall pass that lets you get a reservation in the den. Inside the gorgeous dark library, fifteen hundred bottles of whiskey line walls with rolling ladders. Skilled bartenders make you any manner of drink tableside with a bar cart rolled up right to you for the frostiest drink around, and the dinner menu is banger after banger. This is a seductive spot, and you'll feel it.

But let's say that all sounds too much. Or maybe your drinking days are behind you. No prob, friend, right next door is a Mediterranean gem, **Lil' Shalom**. Bright sumac, feta, and tomato salads. Kebabs that have legions of loyal fans. And squishy hot pita served right from the oven. It's always a win.

Wake up Sunday morning and there are still things to do before catching the train back home. Leave your bags with the front desk so you're unencumbered by silly checkout times. Then get thee selves to longtime brunch fave **Screen Door**'s new Pearl District location. Load up on an order of biscuits and gravy (sausage or mushroom gravy options!) and be ready to mosey out fuller than on Thanksgiving. Walk it off with a stop into **MadeHere PDX**—an entire store stocked with Portland makers selling everything from local nail polish brands to fancy chocolates to high-end leather goods. Right across the street from the shop is the iconic **Powell's Books**, which is always worth a visit.

One more stop on your way back to Union Station (and right around the corner from The Hoxton) is **Deadstock Coffee** for a dope espresso and to see where all the sneaker aficionados in the neighborhood hang out (and there are a lot of them since it's next to **Pensole Footwear Design Academy**). After all the walking, shopping, talking, and eating, you'll want one more coffee for the road. And yes, it is the sign of a successful date if you both want to just nap on the train ride home.

More Fun

If you're looking to get out of downtown, here's a smattering of dates from Portland's five quadrants. Yes, five. That's how weird they are.

NORTH—Portland could be called Brunch City, and there's no better nosh than **Sweedeedee**, named after a song by local legend, Michael Hurley. Find his albums next door at indier-than-indie (and cash only) **Mississippi Records**.

NORTHEAST—Hidden haunts that serve weird wine? Yes, please! Down a nondescript alley off Alberta Street, discover a converted dumpster nook called **Les Clos** and, underground, its dimly lit sister bar, **Les Caves**.

SOUTHEAST—If rain dampens your visit, which it very likely will, book a couple hours at Portland's Scandinavian-style sauna **Löyly**. Keep the trend going with ebelskivers and aquavit at **Broder Café** just up the street.

SOUTHWEST—Washington Park touts 410 acres of secret gardens and wooded paths, but on a clear day, head to the **International Rose Test Garden**, home to more than ten thousand (!!!) varieties of the glamorous bloom, not to mention the best views of downtown and Mount Hood.

NORTHWEST—Each September, join the throngs of picnickers on the hillside of Chapman Elementary School as upwards of thirty thousand **tiny vaux's swifts** swarm the sky before morphing into a cartoonish funnel and diving into the school's brick chimney to roost for the night. It's as unreal as it sounds.

Olympic Loop

When it comes to the biggest bang for your buck, you simply can't beat the four distinct regions of Olympic National Park. Lush, enchanting rain forests creep right up to pensive Pacific beaches, and epic alpine peaks slope back to the Sound, where picturesque fishing villages from bygone eras dot the peninsula's drier east side. While this chapter is laid out as a single loop, consider committing to multiple treks, going deep on each region and giving yourselves the time to fully immerse in the sheer magnitude of beauty that blesses our Wild West.

OLYMPIC GAMES

The four-hundred-ish-mile Olympic Peninsula Loop that swirls from Seattle around the northwest peninsula and back takes you through forests and hot springs, past beaches and lakes, and through adorable Victorian towns. It also takes severallll hours, and we recommend a three-night trip to break up the drive and enjoy what each leg has to offer.

Day one, take off from Seattle and head to **Lake Quinault Lodge** in the Olympic National Forest. The looming lodge is somehow both rustic and stately with green leather sofas in front of a ten-foot-tall brick fireplace, and cozy lakeside rooms. Pay a visit to the glass case in the back corner that houses plaster castings of the various Big Feet (ya know, from Bigfoot) they've found in the area. Then wander outside on the deck to take in the beauty of the lake. Grab Adirondacks for two on the expansive lawn with its famous colorful rain gauge, sip some wine from the bar, and take a deep breath. A **sunset cruise** departing from the lodge's dock most summer nights really blows off the city stress.

On day two, prepare for peace and views and peaceful views. Grab a super-simple breakfast with a lovely, yup, view at Kalaloch Lodge's **Creekside Restaurant** about a half hour away. The menu might be small, but the, um, view of the ocean is mighty. Then onto the **Hoh Rain Forest**, which is not only one of the largest temperate rain forests in the country, it is also, quite literally, the quietest.

An independent research project for Earth Day 2005 declared a spot 3.2 miles from the visitor's center above Mount Tom Creek Meadows on the Hoh River Trail as **One Square Inch of Silence** and likely the quietest place in America. If you're so inclined to find this respite, it's at N 48.12885°, W 123.68234°, and marked by a little red stone on top of a mossy log. Take a moment and listen to what the sound of silence really is. Take that, Simon and Garfunkel! Before you leave the area (or skip straight to it), walk the short **Hall of Mosses** trail, where green bits dramatically sway from towering trees and banana slugs slow roll their way across the path. Then on to **Sol Duc Hot Springs Resort**!

Technically, you can stay the night here, but we recommend dipping in for a soak and moving on. For less than twenty dollars, obtain a day pass, which grants you ninety minutes in the resort's gated area. There, split your time between the three mineral pools that range in temps from a tepid 99 degrees to a more toasty 104. Adjacent to the pools is a swimming-pool-size freshwater pool which, depending on the season, can go from a cold plunge 55 degrees to a refreshing 85.

Sol Duc comes from the Quileute word for "sparkling water," and its healing waters have been known for generations further back than we have record. Rain and melted snow fill the spring, which trickles through the cracks into the sedimentary rocks. Then it gets heated by gasses from volcanic rock, rising to the surface in another crack. Boom, nature's hot tub.

HOT TIP: If you'd rather dive into nature for a fraction of the price, consider camping at Kalaloch Campground. *Sunset* magazine declared camping location D25 the best spot in all the Olympic National Forest for its fabulous 160-degree ocean view.

Now you're off for a lovely dinner and stay at **Lake Crescent Lodge**. The on-site restaurant overlooks the lake, and it's particularly dreamy when the light bounces off the water at sunset. The food is not just good because it's the only option around, but it's legitimately delicious with a menu focused on Northwest fare. As is common with these old lodges, the rooms come with paper-thin walls, so perhaps they aren't ideal if your evening activities (wink) lean on the loud side. If aural freedom is high on the list, spring for one of the adorable cottages or guest rooms outside the main lodge.

Ah, and now it is morning of day three. Awake with a gorgeous crystal clear lake carved by glaciers right in front of you. Stare at the water as you sip coffee with a blanket around your shoulders like an IRL Folgers ad. Before you get back on the road, consider a brisk morning swim or a half-day canoe rental from the lodge's dock. Paddle out into the calm waters and see if you can spot Lake Crescent's famous Beardslee trout. This type of rainbow trout is only found here, and it's fun to see them jumping up from the water to catch a bug snack.

That afternoon, roll through the purple explosions of Sequim's **Lavender Trail**. Consisting of a handful of family farms, the area is known as "America's Provence" for its decidedly Frenchy aesthetic (and smell). You can run through the purple fields, eat lavender ice cream, stock up on bath bombs, or simply quickly drive through to your final night's accommodations in Port Townsend.

Port Townsend is ridiculously charming, with its three hundred picturesque nineteenth-century Victorian homes, built back when everyone was convinced that the town would be the most swinging, popular port and hub in all the state. The railroad derailed that dream, but the lovely port town remains for an ideal romantic stroll. Stay in the thick of things, namely on Water Street at the historic **Palace Hotel**. Built in 1889, this charismatic three-story brick hotel has an infamous history as a brothel founded in the Roaring '20s with a number of ladies working under head madam, Miss Marie.

The gals may be all long gone (although some claim their spirits still pop up for a visit from time to time), but you can rent rooms named after them

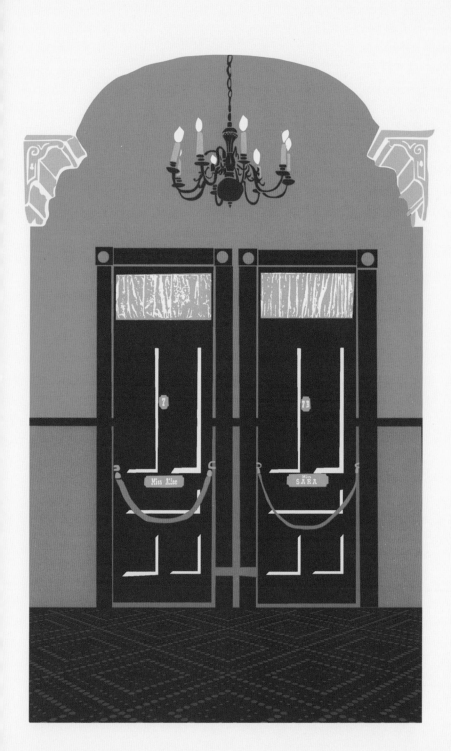

with décor that's era appropriate. The doors have signs with names like "Miss Kitty" and "Miss Pearl," but we suggest choosing "Marie's Suite," with its burgundy carpets, walls, fireplace, and fringed lamps. A corner room means you can lay in bed and watch sailboats drift by out of two sets of windows. One note: prep your glutes because there is no elevator in this historic place, so stairs are required.

After you're checked in, your evening is as simple as going for a wander along the adorable waterfront. There are restaurants to fit any mood, and great Italian ices from **Elevated Ice Cream**. Up for a nightcap? Stop into the swanky bar **The In Between** for artful cocktails and equally inspiring mocktails.

On your last morning of #olympiclooplife, take a short drive to **Fort Worden**. A century ago, you'd have found one thousand troops on the grounds protecting the Puget Sound from attackers. Now it's a 432-acre park with miles of shoreline, restored officer quarters you can sleep in, and all kinds of family fun and festivals. It also might look familiar for anyone who loves *An Officer and a Gentleman,* as the navy wouldn't grant permission for the studio to film on an active base, so they set up camp here.

One more stop for lunch on the road home: the little hamlet of Port Gamble. Once a booming mill town founded by a New England timber company in the mid-1800s, the mill closed in the 1990s, and it dropped down to a double-digit population. Now, it is a cute tourist draw with lovely old homes and a small, walkable main street. Pop into the little shops on North Rainier Avenue and read the plaques with each home's history along the way. Check out loads of goods from the **Port Gamble General Store**, then grab lunch next door at **Scratch Kitchen**. Hit the road with a full belly, and maybe a full heart, too.

More Fun

SUPERSHUCKERS— Depending on how you drive the Olympic Loop, it's easy to miss the Hama Hama Oyster Saloon situated on the banks of the Hood Canal, but this aphrodisiac dealer known for some of the freshest, cleanest, and most iconic oysters on the planet is worth an outing of its own. Reserve ahead for the best picnic ever.

MAGIC GLAMP—If you're looking to spend a little more time on Hood Canal, consider booking a night or two at **Iliana's Glamping Village at Mike's Beach Resort**. Two vintage RVs and eleven tricked-out safari tents provide quirky accommodations for those of us who can't bear to stay in another musty old motel.

TOO SHI SHI, HUSH-HUSH, EYE TO EYE—At the very northwestern tip of the state, on Makah tribal land, you'll find four miles of boardwalk trails that'll deliver you to dramatic views of the rugged coast (get a recreation pass from the Hobuck campground or Neah Bay gas station). Backpack in, pitch a tent right on **Shi Shi Beach**, and settle in for a show—this remote corner has some of the darkest skies in the state, meaning also the brightest stars.

RIDE OFF INTO THE SUNSET—At just over two hours from Seattle, **Ocean Shores** will be the closest option for watching the sun set over the Pacific. Drive your car right onto the sand and scout a perfect spot to pop the trunk and unfurl a sweeping seaside spread.

WHERE HAVE ALL THE MERRYMAKERS GONE?— Each year, the wacky **Port Townsend Bay Kinetic Sculpture Race** hosts two days of human-powered, artistically enhanced vehicles laboring through sand, mud, water, and the picturesque streets of the city. It's fun to be an onlooker, but power couples should consider entering.

Royal Isle

Victoria is named after the queen, so it's no wonder the activities on this illustrious isle conjure majesty and grandeur. Treat yourself like royalty with tea service at a storied hotel, stroll through opulent gardens, and get pampered at a luxurious seaside spa. Blimey! You could even stay in a bloody castle if you want to go all out. And why shouldn't you? Life is short. Love is rad. And these bangers aren't gonna mash themselves.

BUTCHART BETTER GET MY MONEY

There is one destination any good trip to Victoria must incorporate, the internationally renowned **Butchart Gardens**. You've likely heard the name before, but if you've never experienced the rainbow explosion of blooms from this gorgeous place, go. It's fifty-five acres of nature at its absolute prettiest, thanks to the foresight of Jennie Butchart, who began developing the garden in 1904.

There are many things that make this place feel wondrous (the *Alice in Wonderland*–like feel of the blooming begonias, for instance), but one major factor is the distinct "rooms" the estate created with each different garden. A favorite is the **Sunken Garden**, crafted from an old limestone quarry where a central limestone mound still stands and provides an excellent vantage point. The five-acre garden section took nine years to develop, but now visitors can roll through 151 flower beds bursting with 65,000 spring flower bulbs, finding it hard to imagine it was ever a dusty old quarry. You like roses? The **Rose Garden** not only boasts 280 variety of roses, there are 30 dreamy rose arch-ways to practice wedding processions.

Before arriving at the gardens, be sure to make a reservation for **The Dining Room Restaurant** for afternoon tea in the original Butchart family residence. It can accommodate most meal preferences from gluten-free to vegan with advance notice. Take a pause midway through the long day (allow at least four hours just for garden roaming) to load up on things like English trifle with Chantilly cream, baked lemon custard, and little finger sandwiches with chick-pea, pickled apple, walnuts, and fig aioli. Wash it all down with Chinese black and sencha tea infused with bergamot, rhubarb, and blue cornflowers. If you ever played tea party as a child, this is the date of your dreams.

SPA-LA-LA

The **Oak Bay Beach Hotel** has no shortage of views. From pink-hued sunrises with Mount Baker in the distance to watching birds soar over the Salish Sea, it's the royal flush of destinations. It was awarded the number-one spot for Canadian hotels in the Condé Nast 2021 Readers' Choice Awards (also named one of the most romantic by Tripadvisor folks). And for good reason.

Each one of the hundred rooms features in-room fireplaces, floor-to-ceiling windows, and fuzzy bathrobes. Slip one on and head down to three mineral pools butted up against the sea. Each are heated year-round for a nice swim, no matter the season. Lounge in the **Boathouse Kitchen & Bar** with a cocktail in hand, a warm pool at your toes, and the cold sea in sight.

Let's say you already have accommodations elsewhere but that pool sitch sounds enticing? We got you. Book a service right next to the pools at the lauded **Boathouse Spa**, like a deep tissue massage or the hyaluronic acid and collagen facial. Any spa service includes the option to upgrade for a rea-sonable fee to add two hours of access to the mineral pools so you can enjoy all the perks whether you have a room key or not.

Whichever way you dip into those pools, dip into the olde English pub **Penny Farthing** after. Utterly winsome, with plaid wallpaper, crackling fireplaces, and overall Victorian charm, its décor is on point and its fare is casual. There's the requisite pub fish-and-chips and Ploughman's Lunch alongside salads and flatbreads, not to mention a lengthy beer list that includes Guinness, for the full (literally and figuratively) pub experience.

TICKLE YOUR PICKLE

Have you ever heard of a pickle boat? It is perhaps the cutest name of all the boats; hop on one for a **Harbour Tour** in Victoria Harbour. Only a handful of boaters fit on these little guys for a forty-five-minute tour. Learn about the sacred territories of First Nation people, witness colorful seaplanes coming in for a landing, and maybe even spot a cute little sea otter looking like a kitty that fell in a bathtub. If you're visiting on a weekend from April to October, be at the waterfront in the morning to witness the pickle boats and their famous **Water Ballet**. When the little crafts arrived in 1990, the skippers couldn't believe their ability to twist and turn, deciding to really show off their skills by choreograph-ing an intricate multi-boat dance where they spin in circles, swirl in and out of figure eights, and seem to come to life like ballerinas on the stage. Magic.

Back on dry land, take a few minutes to walk to **Chinatown**. Victoria's Chinatown is the oldest in Canada, and one of the oldest in North America, due to tens of thousands of Chinese gold miners and railroad workers coming through the area between the 1850s and 1880s. The neighborhood has contin-ued to cultivate an active community for residents and visitors over the decades and is a wonderful place for a stroll. There's the famed **Fan Tan Alley**, known for being the narrowest street in Canada. Now it's full of shops and informative

plaques and photos of the immigrants who once lived here, preserving their heritage and educating visitors on their experience.

A great place to stock up on more history, or on any topic, for that matter, is the independent **Munro's Books** located inside the stately old Royal Bank Building. Founded in 1963 by Nobel Prize–winning author Alice Munro and her then husband Jim, it's been a spot for book lovers for sixty years. It might be one of the prettiest bookstores you'll ever visit, and its huge inventory (including a sizable children's section) is worthy of your time.

Wrap up the day with a trek down a little hallway that gives way to the brick speakeasy of **Little Jumbo Restaurant & Bar**. Every handful of weeks, they deliver an entirely new set of delicious craft cocktails, alongside the classics. The libations are reason enough to pop in, but the fresh seasonal menu that rotates—think grilled Caesar wedge salads, morel gnocchi, and fresh fish—means you can sit and stay a spell.

GOOD THINGS COME IN
SMALL PACKAGES

You know what afternoon tea is about, right? Tiny cups of delicious fragrant tea, teeny sandwiches with layers of cream cheese and cucumber, and itty-bitty fruity desserts piled on a tray. It's freakin' delightful. If you want your cuppa with a side of tradition, go for **tea at the Fairmont Empress hotel**.

For more than a hundred years, guests have flocked to the hotel's sophisticated lobby lounge, replete with stately columns and potted palms, to indulge in afternoon tea. Here's how it goes: A finely dressed server arrives with hot teas wafting floral scents right up into the tickly part of your nose. Then come rounds and rounds of little snacks that somehow manage to satisfy a big appetite. There are, of course, the aforementioned sandwiches like cold smoked sockeye salmon with chive crème fraîche and egg salad on sourdough. Then comes the tiered tray of sweetness. Fresh scones with clotted cream, strawberry rose macarons, Empress honey, and lavender shortbread. Cocktails made with color-changing purple gin. The tea experience may not be cheap, but it's worth every loonie and toonie.

As long as you're enamored with diminutive things, consider a total vibe switch from the ritzy tea to teeny displays of history at **Miniature World**. Located in the back corner of the hotel, the attraction is quirky as can be. With eighty-five intricately detailed dioramas all waist high, it's hard to imagine the time and effort that went into building these little worlds. View a *Swiss Family Robinson* display with thatched roof tree houses barely bigger than a hand surrounded by an entire tropical forest. Check out historic displays, such as a mini swinging London with carefully built double-decker buses. This jewel box of a place also features the world's smallest operational sawmill. It's a surprising amount of fun for both kids and grown-ups alike.

A WALK IN THE PARK

A simple luxury during a weekend away is *time*, the time to have a leisurely meal and long walk to really talk. Without interruptions from texts, Slack, human or fur children, chores, and adulting writ large. This day is all about taking it slow and catching up. Embark with brunch at **10 Acres Bistro**.

The farm-to-table restaurant means the philosophy quite literally manifests through growing a large portion of the menu at their 10 Acres Farm, where vegetables are grown primarily from heirloom seeds. They also have an orchard of fruit and nut trees like apricots and hazelnuts with an apiary on-site for bees to help pollinate the fruit, which is made into fresh chutneys and ice cream. Sit on the plant-filled patio and tuck into the freshest omelet and salad around.

Then start walking. In this case, toward the two-hundred-acre beauty of **Beacon Hill Park**. It has a bit of everything, making it perfect for a long wander. You might see the park's pride of peacocks cruising around with the males showing off their jewel-toned feathers. There's a coastal section where kite flyers soar their colorful creations and the occasional paraglider happens by. Walk over the little stone bridges and watch the ducks paddle in the ponds. With all this languid serenity, take time to talk about all your hopes and dreams.

CASTLE PLAY

Victoria feels posh, no way getting around it. Maybe that's why Posh Spice being actually named Victoria makes perfect sense. But the ultimate posh baller move is building your own castle. Which is exactly what coal baron Robert Dunsmuir did.

Dunsmuir started building the **Craigdarroch Castle** in 1887 on the hill overlooking the city in a total flex move to show how much money he had. No one can confirm or deny if he also wanted to swim in piles of gold coins like Scrooge McDuck, but there are thirty-nine rooms in the twenty-five-thousand-square-foot baronial mansion, so it seems possible one could be earmarked for gold swimming. Unfortunately, Robert passed in 1889 before the home was completed, his wife following a few years later. Since then, the castle has had a revolving door of owners. It was a military hospital right after World War I, then a college for two decades before becoming a school board office, and then the Victoria Conservatory of Music in the 1970s. Whew. In 1979, is became the museum it still is today, allowing visitors to observe its glorious stained glass and imagine what luxury life was like back in the day.

You can stay in a nearby mansion as well, by booking a room at the century-old Italian mansion turned bed-and-breakfast, **Fairholme Manor Inn**. With jetted tubs, romantic fireplaces, and an acre of beautiful gardens, this is a solid choice for those reasons alone. But the breakfasts are beloved. They've racked up enough attention and so many press mentions, the inn had to put out a cookbook to reveal the secrets behind favorites like baked raspberry French toast.

Acknowledgments

We could not have made this book, or be the people we are, without a killer set of friends. Thank you to Matt Beebe for letting Eden crash on all your couches over the years (and to Tymberly Seim for being a copilot on all those drives). We are lucky to call you all family. To Spiral Stairs for luring Ashod to Seattle, Erin Waters Lightfoot for sharing your love of the city, and to two favorites who are no longer with us, Aaron Huffman and Darius Minwalla. Your joyful spirits will always haunt these streets.

To Rachel Demy and Benjamin Gibbard, thank you for letting us set up camp at your place while we were deep in research mode and for the late-night talks full of useful tips. To Laura Gibson, for being our self-assigned intrepid reporter, always taking the best notes for us. To Liza Rietz, for letting us mine her childhood for ideas. To Dave Depper and Julia Austin, for getting stuck in a snowstorm and sharing all the goods with us. To Josh Meyer, for enthusiastic San Juan Islands tips. To Kelly Coller and Tony Secolo, for coming back into Ashod's life just when he needed them (and a couch to sleep on).

To Heather Brooks Rensmith, our couple's therapist. We'd have no way of understanding how to navigate being in love, writing books together, running businesses together, eking our way through the onslaught of life, and juggling our dramatic duo Leo ways without someone giving us some great guidance along the way. Thank you.

Giant hugs to all our friends and family for encouraging us as the deadline drew near and to our Joshua Tree family for always being in our hearts.

Thank you to Rena Priest for helping us make sure our words were inclusive and to Danika Nalo for all her research support. A huge-ass thank you to all the Sasquatch crew: Jen Worick for being our cheerleader and an utter delight, Michelle Hope for being the best freaking copyeditor in the game, Isabella Hardie for keeping us on deadline, Tony Ong for taking files upon files and turning them into gorgeous pages, and Nikki Sprinkle for finding it actual readers!

We couldn't have gone on all these adventures without the local publications that tirelessly write about this beautiful state. Support regional journalism. You won't know what you got 'til it's gone.

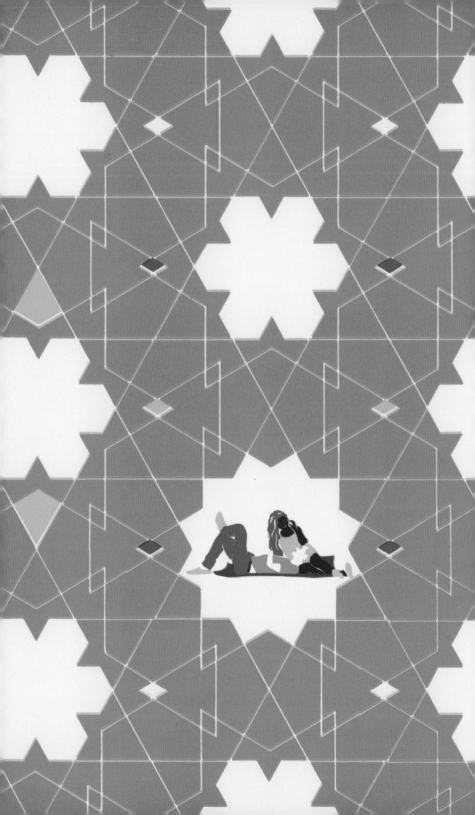

Cheat Sheet

First Date

Let's French 2

Sir Mix-a-Latte 7

Celebrate Happiness 10

Such Great Heights 19

Garden of Stone 53

Soul Mates 54

Group Date

Old-Fashioned Fun 6

Belly Laughs 7

Keep It Like a Secret 23

Bar Crossed Lovers 33

Tasting Menu 49

Express Yourself 54

Special Occasions

The Big O 3

Goes Down Like a
Fine Wine 45

Temple of the ~~Dog~~ Elk 58

Duck Duck Soup 82

(Leaven)worth It 100

Audrey Horne-y 103

Spa-La-La 137

Cheap Dates

Moonrise Kingdom 4

Grease the Wheels 7

Woo Your Date 9

Be Kind Rewind 18

Kidding Around 24

"It's the Water" 110

Romance Novel Dates

Smokin' Hot 34

Wild Wild West 43

Aye-Aye, Captain 73

I Wanna Hold
Your Chelan 102

Hot and Heavy 117

Regulators Mount Up 122

Ride Off into the Sunset 135

For a Hang with Your Friend

Let's Have a Ball 10

Good Times,
Great Oldies 26

Easy Does It 43

Tiptoe through
the Tulips 68

Plan B 124

Solo Dates

Manual Stimulation 15

Vinyl Fling 16

Dog Day Afternoon 24

You Look Georgeous 51

PDA in PDX 125

Tickle Your Pickle 138

Take the Kids Too

Carkeeks and Geeks 38

Doll Parts 40

Go H.A.M. 69

Fiesta Forever 86

Joust the Two of Us 104

Good Things Come
in Small Packages 141

When Your Parents Are Visiting

Get High on History! 8

A Green Fall 26

The Birds and the ~~Bees~~ Fish 30

For Old Time's Sake 47

Garden Variety 83

A Fourth to Be Reckoned With 105

Water Lovers

Mezcal Float 21

Bay Watch 31

Little Mermaids 39

Easy Does It 43

Hit the Road, Jacques 116

Better Yourself 121

Olympic Games 130

Queer Approved

Will You Be My Sweatheart? 4

Eat, Drink, and Be Gay 14

Manual Stimulation 15

Good Times, Great Oldies 26

Get It, Grrrl 113

PDA in PDX 125

Foodies

What's Cookin', Good Lookin'? 29

Goes Down Like a Fine Wine 45

Tasting Menu 49

Happy Trails 91

Farmer Fun 123

Supershuckers 135

Hikes

Wake-n-Lake 67

Go H.A.M. 69

Orcas Porcus 76

#2 Best Hike 105

Two Tickets to Paradise 106

"It's the Water" 110

Olympic Games 130

Too Shi Shi, Hush-Hush,
Eye to Eye 135

Flora Fans

In Bloom 22

Garden of Stone 53

That's a Good Point 63

Tiptoe through
the Tulips 68

Garden Variety 83

Golden Hour 94

Byway to Heaven 111

Butchart Better
Get My Money 136

Fauna Fans

Dog Day Afternoon 24

It's Friday (Harbor)
and I'm in Love 79

Stanley Tucci My Body 92

Two Tickets to Paradise 106

Byway to Heaven 111

Hit the Road, Jacques 116

A Walk in the Park 141

Rainy Days

The Art of Making Out 7

Classic Movie Night 22

What's Cookin',
Good Lookin'? 29

Magic Your Gathering 33

Sparks Are Flying 52

Temple of the ~~Dog~~ Elk 58

Spring

Vinyl Fling 16

In Bloom 22

The Birds and the
~~Bees~~ Fish 30

Wham Bam Thank
You Clam 62

Tiptoe through
the Tulips 68

Faked Alaska 105

Summer

Westward, Ho! 29

Bay Watch 31

Wild Wild West 43

That's a Good Point 63

Range Life 96

I Wanna Hold
Your Chelan 102

Fall

A Green Fall 26

Too Bright 29

Carkeeks and Geeks 38

Garden of Stone 53

Baby, You Can
Drive My Car 70

Where Have All the
Merrymakers Gone? 135

Winter

Will You Be My
Sweatheart? 4

Tropical Punch 13

Adrenaline Crush 94

Range Life 96

(Leaven)worth It 100

I Will Follow You
Into the Dark 118

Index

A

Add-a-Ball arcade, 24
Agua Verde Cafe & Paddle Club, 21
Aladdin's Antiques and Records (aka
    Aladdin's Lamp), 69
Alki Avenue Flower Houses, 43
Alki Beach, 43
Alki Point Lighthouse, 43
Alma, 65
Amtrak's Coast Starlight train, 125
Archie McPhee, 24
Arts Club Theatre Company, 91
Asian Family Market, 49
Azalea Way at Washington Park
    Arboretum UW Botanic Gardens,
    16–17

B

Baby Goat Yoga, 122–123
Backdoor at Roxy's, The, 23
Bagley Lakes Loop, 68
Bainbridge, 84–86
Ballard, 30–35
Ballard (Hiram M. Chittenden) Locks,
    30–31
Ballyhoo Curiosity Shop, 33
Banya 5, 4
Barking Frog, 45
Bathtub Gin & Co, 3
Beacon Hill Park, 142
Belle Epicurean Bakery, 16
Bellingham, 69–70
Bizzarro Italian Cafe, 24
Blackcomb ski resort, 118–120
Bloedel Reserve, 84–86
Blue Sky Outfitters, 101
Boathouse Kitchen & Bar, 137
Boathouse Spa, 137–138
Bob's Java Jive, 65
Book Larder, 29
Books Kinokuniya, 11

Bors Hede Inne, 104
Bow and Edison, 70
Bow Hill Blueberries, 70
Boxcar Park, 41
Breadfarm, 70
Bremerton, 84, 86
Bremerton Community Theater, 86
Brewery Park at Tumwater Falls, 110–111
British Columbia, 90–95, 116–120,
    136–143
Brockton Point totem poles, 93
Broder Café, 129
Brothers Greenhouses, 84
Burke-Gilman Trail, 25
Butchart Gardens, 136–137

C

Café Turko, 29
Caffe Vita, 7
Cake House, 9
Calico Cupboard, 69
Camlann Medieval Village, 104
Can Can Culinary Cabaret, 2–3
Canyon Lights, 95
Capilano Suspension Bridge Park,
    94–95
Capitol Hill, 13–17
Captain Whidbey Inn, 73–74
Carkeek Park, 38
Carl S. English Jr. Botanical Garden,
    30–31
Cascadian Home Farm Stand, 96
Cave B Estate Winery, 124
Central Cinema, 16
Central Library, 3
cherry blossom trees, 22
Chinatown (Victoria), 138–139
Chuckanut Drive, 70
ChuMinh Tofu and Vegan Deli, 10
Cliffwalk, 95
Colman Pool, 43–44
Copper Creek Inn, 109

Coupeville, 74
Cove, The, 74
Craigdarroch Castle, 142
Cranberry Lake, 76
Creekside Restaurant, 130
Crystal Ballroom, 125

D

Dahlia Trial Garden, 64
Damaged Room, 51
Danner, 127
Danny Woo Community Garden, 9
Darcelle XV, 125
Darvill's Bookstore, 76
dates, cheat sheet for, 147–151
Deadstock Coffee, 128
Deception Pass, 74–76
Deck, The, 46
DeLille Cellars, 46
Derby Pond, 70
Devil's Reef, 61
Dining Room Restaurant, The, 137
Discovery Bikes, 103
Dockside Cannabis, 29
Dockside Restaurant, 91
Doc's Bar, 60
Doe Bay Fest, 77
Downtown Seattle, 2–7
Downtown Yakima Farmers Market, 123
Dragonfest, 11
Duck Soup, 82
Dumpling Trail, 91–92

E

East Side, 45–49
Eastern Washington, 121–124
Easy Street Cafe, 44
Easy Street Records, 44
Eatonville, 106–107
Edmonds Underwater Park, 39
Edmonds Underwater Sports, 39
Elandan Gardens, 84
Elevated Ice Cream, 134
Elks Lodge #827, 31
Elliott Bay Book Company, 15
Evergreen State College, 113

F

Fairholme Manor Inn, 142
Fairmont Empress hotel, tea at, 141
Fairmont Olympic Hotel, 3
Fan Tan Alley, 138–139
Fantagraphics Bookstore & Gallery, 51
ferries, 71
Fireside Lounge, 45
First Nations art and totem poles, 93
Flower Houses on Alki Avenue, 43
Fonda La Catrina, 51
Fort Nisqually, 63–64
Fort Worden, 134
Frances May, 127
Fremont, 23–29
Fremont Solstice Parade, 28
Fremont Sunday Market, 28
Fremont Vintage Mall, 28
Friday Harbor, 79–80
Funko Pop Headquarters, 40
Fuzhou Ting, 62

G

Gas Works Park, 25
Georgetown Records, 51
Georgetown Trailer Park Mall, 51
Geraldine's Counter, 54
Glacier Public Service Center, 67
Golden Gardens Park, 34
Gorge Amphitheater, 124
Graduate Seattle hotel, 21
Grand Farm, 87
Grand Illusion Cinema, 22
Grand Pavilion, 11
Granville Island Public Market, 90–91
Great Carnation 4th of July
    Celebration, 105
Green Lake, 26, 29
Greenlake Boathouse, 26
Grove of the Patriarchs, 109

H

Hall of Mosses, 131
Hama Hama Oyster Saloon, 135
Harbor Lights, 63

Harbour Tour, 138
Hattie's Hat, 33
Hazlewood, 33
Heather Meadows, 68
Hedges Family Estate Winery, 122
Henry Art Gallery, 19
Hing Hay Park, 11
Hobbit House, 84
Hoh Rain Forest, 130–131
Hollywood Tavern, 47
Hot Tub Boat, 6
Hotel Pension Anna, 101
Hound + Bottle, 86
Howe Sound, 116, 117
Hoxton, The, 125
Hyper Market, 28

I

iFly, 52
Iliana's Glamping Village at Mike's
  Beach Resort, 135
Imperfetta, 25
In Between, The, 134
Inside Passage, 13
International District, 8–11
International Rose Test Garden, 129
Island Soul Rum Bar & Soul Shack, 55
Islands of the North, 72–82
Islands of the South, 83–87

J

Jack's Fish Spot and Crab Pot, 7
James Turrell Skyspace, 19
Japanese Garden, 86
John S. McMillin Memorial
  Mausoleum, 82

K

K Fresh, 41
Kalaloch Campground, 132
Kangaroo House Bed & Breakfast, 77
Kerry Park, 4
KEXP, 7
Kiana Lodge, 103

Klahanie Campground, 117
Klondike Gold Rush National Historic
  Park, 8
Kubota Garden, 53–54

L

Laburnum Walk, 94
Lake Chelan Boat Company, 102
Lake Crescent Lodge, 132
Lake Quinault Lodge, 130
Lan Su Chinese Garden, 127
Larrabee State Park, 70
Lavender Trail, 132
Leavenworth, 100–101
Leavenworth Alphorns, 101
Les Caves, 129
Les Clos, 129
Lil' Shalom, 128
Lime Kiln Point, 80
Lincoln Park, 43–44
Little Jumbo Restaurant & Bar, 139
Little Red Hen Bakery, 74
Lockspot Cafe, 30
Locurio, 23
Lopez Island, 82
Los Hernández Tamales, 123
Löyly, 129
Lucca, 33
Luminata, 29
Lunar New Year celebrations, 11

M

Machus, 127
MadeHere PDX, 128
Madison, 13–17
Madison Park, 17
Madrona, 13–17
Magdalena's Bistro and Crêperie, 70
Magnolia, 2–7
Maiden of Deception Pass, 76
Maneki, 11
maps, x–xi, 1, 37, 57, 89, 115
Marination Ma Kai, 43
Mariners game, 10
Marrakesh, 7
Masquers Theater, 121–122

Matia, 79
Maurice, 127
Maximilien restaurant, 2
Mazama General Store, 98
McMenamins Elks Temple, 58–60
Mill Haus Cider Co., 106–107
Mima Mounds, 111
Miniature World, 141
Mississippi Records, 129
Molly Moon, 4
MonGa Café, 49
Moss Bay, 6
Moss Garden, 86
Mount Baker, 67–68
Mount Constitution, 79
Mount Rainier, 106–109
Mountain Lake, 79
Mountaineering Club, 21
Movie Cat Trivia, 16
Mox Boarding House, 34
Multnomah Whiskey Library, 127–128
München Haus, 101
Munro's Books, 139
Museum of Museums, 15–16
My Haunted Forest, 87

N

Nisqually Vista Trail, 107
North Cascades, 96–99
North Cascades Lodge, 102
North Cascades Scenic Byway, 96
North Fork Brewery, Pizzeria and Beer
    Shrine, 68
North Lake, 23–29
North of Seattle, 38–41
Northern Exposure, 105
Northwest Trek Wildlife Park, 106
Novelty Hill-Januik Winery, 46

O

Oak Bay Beach Hotel, 137
Ocean Shores, 135
Odyssey, 80
Off the Rez, 19
OL Reign, 10
Old Edison, The, 70

Old Hangout, 60
Old Schoolhouse Brewery, 98
Old Town Cafe, 69
Olympia, 110–113
Olympia Timberland Library, 113
Olympic Bar, 3
Olympic Loop, 130–135
One Square Inch of Silence, 131
Opera Alley, 60
Orcas Hotel's Jazz Supper Club, 82
Orcas Island, 76–79, 82
Orcas Island Pottery, 76
Orient Express, 54
Outlook Inn, 76–77
Over the Moon Cafe, 60
Övn Wood Fired Pizza, 70
Oxford Saloon, 47–48

P

Packwood's Labor Day Flea Market, 109
Palace Hotel, 132–134
Pam Rocks, 116
Paradise Inn, 107
Parsons Garden, 4
Peak 2 Peak Gondola, 120
Pebble Cove Farm Inn and Animal
    Sanctuary, 77
Penny Farthing, 138
Penny Lane Antique Mall, 69
Pensole Footwear Design Academy, 128
Picture Lake, 67–68
Pidgin, 94
Pie Bar, 33
Pike/Pine, 13–17
Pioneer Square, 8–11
Piper's Orchard, 38
Point Atkinson Lighthouse, 116
Point Defiance Marina, 64
Point Defiance Park, 63–64
Point Ruston Farmers Market, 63
Pony, 14
Poo Poo Point, 105
Porchlight Coffee & Records, 16
Port Gamble General Store, 134
Port Orchard, 84
Port Townsend, 132–134
Port Townsend Bay Kinetic Sculpture
    Race, 135
Portland, Oregon, 125–129

Posthotel, 101
Powell's Books, 128
Procession of the Species, 112
Prosser Farmers Market, 123

Q

Queen Anne, 2–7
Queer/Bar, 14

R

Rainbow Falls, 103
Rainy Day Records, 113
Ray's Café, 31
Red Hall, 3
Red Mountain Trails Winery, 122–123
Reflection Pool, 86
Rendezvous, 120
Resilient Hearts Animal Sanctuary, 25
Richmond Night Market, 92
Ristorante Machiavelli, 16
River's Edge Resort, 98
Road to Paradise, The, 107
Roozengaarde, 69
Rosario Beach tide pools, 74–76
Rosario Marina, 79
Rosario Resort & Spa, 79
Rose Cole Yelton Memorial Pole, 93
Rose Garden (Vancouver), 93
Rose Garden (Victoria), 137
Roslyn, 105
Ross Lake Resort, 97
Roundhouse Lodge, 120
Roxy's Diner, 26, 28
Royal Room, The, 55
Ruston Way, waterfront path on, 62

S

Sagecliffe Resort & Spa, 124
Sail-in Cinema, 41
Salish Lodge & Spa, 103
San Juan Excursions, 80
San Juan Island, 79–80, 82
Scandinave Spa Whistler, 117–118
Scarecrow Video, 18

Scratch Kitchen, 134
Screen Door, 128
Sea to Sky Gondola, 117
Sea to Sky Highway, 116–120
Seafair Milk Carton Derby, 26
Seattle Art Museum, 7
Secret Cove, 82
Setsunai Noodle Bar, 82
Seward Park, 54
Sewell's Marina, 116
Shakespeare Garden, 93
Shannon Falls Provincial Park, 116–117
Shaughnessy Restaurant, 94
Sheri's Sweet Shoppe, 98
Shi Shi Beach, 135
Skagit Valley Tulip Festival, 68–89
Skalka, 4
Skwachàys Lodge Aboriginal Hotel &
     Gallery, 93–94
Sky Pilot Suspension Bridge, 117
Smith Tower Observatory, 8
Smith Tower Observatory Bar, 8–9
Snohomish, 47–48
Snoqualmie Falls, 103
Soap Lake, 121–122
Society Hotel, 125
Sol Duc Hot Springs Resort, 131
Sorrento Hotel's Silent Reading Parties,
     16
Sound Garden, The, 22
South Lake Union, 2–7
South of Seattle, 50–55
South of the Border, 66–70
Spanish Ballroom, 58
Spartacus Leathers, 127
Spicy PoPo, 49
Stadium High School, 65
Stanley Park, 92–93
Stanley Park Train, 93
Star Theater, 125
Stehekin, 102–103
Stehekin Pastry Company, 103
Stonehouse Cafe, The, 53
Strawberry Festival, 87
Sukhothai Restaurant, 49
Sully's Snowgoose Saloon, 26
Sun Mountain Lodge, 98–99
Sunken Garden, 137
Supreme Dumplings, 49
Sweedeedee, 129

T

Tacoma (Tac-Town), 58–65
Tacoma Vintage Walks, 61
Tai Tung, 10
Talaysay Tours, 93
Talking Totems Indigenous Art Tour, 93
Taylor's Shellfish Oyster Bar and
    Shellfish Market, 70
10 Acres Bistro, 141–142
Tenino Quarry Pool, 111
Theatresports, 91
Thornewood Castle, 65
Tides Tavern, 64
Toby's Tavern, 74
Top Pot, 6
Tope, 125
totem poles at Brockton Point, 93
Tour de Forests, 100–105
TreeHouse Point, 105
Treetops Adventure, 95
Twede's Cafe, 103
21 Acres Farm Market, 47
Twin Peaks Tour, 104
Twin Peaks, 103–104

U

U-District, 18–22
Uwajimaya, 11

V

Vallea Lumina, 118
Vancouver, British Columbia, 90–95
Vancouver Studio Glass, 91
Vault, The, 60
vaux's swifts, 129
Venik Night, 4
Victoria, British Columbia, 136–143
Viking Fest, 86
Volunteer Park Conservatory, 13

W

Wallingford, 23–29
Water Ballet, 138

Water Taxi Shuttle #775, 43
Wellspring Spa and Woodland Retreat,
    107–109
West Seattle, 42–44
West Seattle Water Taxi, 43
West Valley U-Pick, 123
Westward, 29
Whatcom Falls Park, 69–70
Wheel Fun Rentals, 43
Whidbey Island Bagel Factory, 74
Whidbey Island, 73–74
Whirlpool Falls, 70
Whistler Pride and Ski Festival, 120
Whistler Summer Concert Series, 120
Whistler Village Beer Festival, 120
Whistler, 117–120
Wildberry Restaurant, 109
Wildfang, 127
WildLanterns, 29
Wildrose, 15
Wildwood Chapel, 96–97
Willows Lodge, 45
Winter Karneval, 101
Winthrop, 98
Winthrop Rink, 98
Wolf Haven, 112
Woodinville Whiskey Co., 47
World Ski & Snowboard Festival, 120

Y

Yakama Nation Fruit & Produce, 123
Yakima Valley, 123

Te Amo

About the Authors

Eden Dawn is an award-winning writer, host, and entrepreneur from Portland, Oregon. She's a beloved local personality, often seen performing at storytelling events, moderating author and design panels, and chatting through live television segments. She is the host of her own quarterly series *Fashion in Film* at Portland's historic Hollywood Theatre, of the live talk show *Bad Dates*, and of the podcast *We Can't Print This*.

Ashod Simonian is a creative director at North, a boutique advertising agency; cofounder of Imaginary Authors, a niche perfume house; and author of *Real Fun*, a book of photography and stories documenting his decade spent touring the world in various indie rock bands.

Together Eden and Ashod run the activism-based nail polish company Claws Out, which has included collaborations with the Portland Trail Blazers and Elizabeth Warren's presidential campaign. They first began publishing the Book of Dates series in 2021 as a natural extension of their adventurous, overextended lifestyle, bringing together Eden's passion for words and Ashod's handcrafted illustrations. They met backstage at a friend's rock show in 2012 and wrote this book from their slightly creaky hundred-year-old house in Portland's Alberta Arts District with their goofball cats, Daphne and Foxglove.